Praise for
Light in Blue Shadows
TRANSFORMING GRIEF

"A universal paean to all mothers' grief at the loss of sons, no matter how they die, their race or class."

Patrice Wynne, author of *The Womanspirit Sourcebook.*

"It is unusual to find a book about tragedy that is both uplifting and enlightening…a book that can't fail to move you."

Susan Page, author of
How One of You Can Bring the Two of You Together

"Hartshorne's warm intelligence guides us through the landscape of grief. The portrait of her family that emerges reminds one of all that is good about families and how uniquely healing they can be."

China Galland, author of
Longing for Darkness, Tara and the Black Madonna

"What happens when…a heart is forced to endure the devastating grief of a mother unexpectedly losing a child? Light in Blue Shadows is the record of such a journey; a tale…with a promise and purity all its own…a blessing for the rest of us."

Peter Levitt, author of *Fingerpainting on the Moon*

"I fell into this heart-rending and uplifting tale and could not stop reading it. It will console anyone who has lost someone dearly loved."

Melody Ermachild Chavis, author of *Altars in the Street*

"Through [Hartshorne's] graceful writing, I easily entered the particular textures of her worlds of music, of traditional Japan, of New England, and spiritual seeking…joining the living and the dead."

Taigen Dan Leighton, author of *Faces of Compassion*

"Hartshorne shows us a way not only to survive but also to flourish. I recommend this delicate and beautiful work to inspire health professionals and help their patients deal with grief."

Dr. David Werdegar, Professor Emeritus,
University of California Medical School;
Former Health Director, City of San Francisco.

"[Hartshorne's] achingly truthful poetic prose will be good food for anyone facing losses."

Lenore Friedman, author of *Meetings with Remarkable Women: Buddhist Teachers in America*

"[An] exquisite piece of work…and a fitting tribute not only to [Hartshorne's] blessed son but also to all of us who love and grieve."

Maria Housden, author of *Hannah's Gift*

"Spare language full of clear tones that strike the heart…a series of vivid prayers, with bell-like visuals."

Kathleen Sweeney, author,
multimedia creator of Maiden USA

"Hartshorne's honest writing takes us into realms of pain and courage and love that can only make our sense of humanity richer and more precious."

Betsy Rose, musician, songwriter: *In My Two Hands*

"Hartshorne guides us, like Dante's Virgil, on…a journey through the levels of hell. But then she takes us through something more precious than Dante's heavenly hierarchy…a true story that reaches so soul-deep…you can't put it down."

Sherry Anderson, co-author of *The Cultural Creatives*

"[Having been] through the fire…[Hartshorne]… kindly, kindly, [is] willing to help others pass through— it is the deepest generosity imaginable."

— Naomi Shihab Nye, author of *Words Under The Words*

Light in
Blue Shadows

TRANSFORMING GRIEF

Light in Blue Shadows

TRANSFORMING GRIEF

Edie Hartshorne

"White Owl Flies Into and Out of the Field," reprinted from *House of Light*, by Mary Oliver, Copyright © 1990. Used with permission of the publisher, Beacon Press, Boston.

"Please Call Me by My True Names," reprinted from *Call Me By My True Names: The Collected Poems of Thich Nhat Hanh* (1999) by Thich Nhat Hanh. Used with permission of Parallax Press, Berkeley California. www.parallax.org

"Kindness," reprinted from *Words Under The Words*, by Naomi Shihab Nye, Far Corner Books, Oregon, 1995. Used with permission of the author, 2006.

"Psalm 30," reprinted from *Opening to You: Zen-Inspired Translations of the Psalms*, by Norman Fischer, Viking Adult, 2002. Used with permission of the author, 2005.

For reasons of privacy, some names of people and places have been changed.

ISBN -13: 978-0-9788699-0-8
ISBN -10: 0-9788699-0-7

Printed in the United States of America

This book is printed on acid-free paper.

Book Design: Kate Canfield

Cover artwork "Mystic Messenger" by Nicholas Kirsten-Honshin, used with permission of the artist. www.honshin.com

Additional copies of this book can be ordered at:
www.lightinblueshadows.com

Ellsberg Books
Berkeley, CA
www.ellsbergbooks.com

To Robin, Ben and Keshi

With gratitude and love

In memoriam

Jonathan Churchill Hartshorne

1972 – 1992

White Owl Flies
Into and Out of the Field

Coming down
out of the freezing sky
with its depths of light,
like an angel,
or a Buddha with wings,
it was beautiful
and accurate,
striking the snow and whatever was there
with a force that left the imprint
of the tips of its wings—
five feet apart—and the grabbing
thrust of its feet,
and the indentation of what had been running
through the white valleys
of the snow—

and then it rose, gracefully,
and flew back to the frozen marshes,
to lurk there,
like a little lighthouse,
in the blue shadows—
so I thought:
maybe death
isn't darkness, after all,
but so much light
wrapping itself around us—

as soft as feathers—
that we are instantly weary
of looking, and looking, and shut our eyes,
not without amazement,
and let ourselves be carried,
as through the translucence of mica,
to the river
that is without the least dapple or shadow—
that is nothing but light—scalding, aortal light—
in which we are washed and washed
out of our bones.

—*Mary Oliver*

Table of Contents

Light in Blue Shadows

TRANSFORMING GRIEF

Prologue

Moonlight

My twelve-year-old son Jonathan yelled from the attic in an excited voice, "Can you come up for a minute?" I was just going out the door for a full afternoon with a rehearsal of my music group and then a gathering of other mothers—close friends who met once a month to chat and celebrate the full moon.

"I'm going to be late for my rehearsal," I called up the stairway. "Can it wait?"

"I want to show you right now. I just finished!" He sounded elated, and I could not resist. I phoned my colleagues and left a message that I would be there soon.

I walked upstairs to the second floor, into Jonathan's room. I opened his closet, the only way up to his hideaway in the attic. Holding onto the top beam, I balanced one foot on the clothes hook and the other on the clothing bar and poked my head up through the ceiling hole in the closet. I blinked, adjusting my eyes to the dim musky attic where Jonathan had built his computer haven.

There were no windows, but the attic was warm and comfortable, and Jonathan had strung up Christmas lights to outline the high beams, where he had hung posters of Star Trek and Darth Vader. He had created a sound system he could activate from his bed below and had built a small fan for hot afternoons, using one of my old hair dryers.

Jonathan took off his earphones when he saw me. He was sitting at his desk in front of the computer, his baseball hat askew, wearing a t-shirt, shorts, and sandals because he refused to wear socks. His knobby bowlegs stuck out on either side of the small desk; his blond hair tufted around the sides of his cap, far below his ears. He rubbed the back of his hand across his nose. "Look!" he said.

Except for the blinking Christmas lights and the bluish glow of the small computer screen, I could see nothing. I sat down beside Jonathan on a wobbly plastic pail he had turned upside down for guests. To me, computer programming still existed as a magical language in another dimension. But Jonathan's enthusiasm delighted me, and his prowess filled me with pride. Sitting close to him in the darkness was as cozy as going to the movies, and I began to make out a small image, which slowly built itself upon the screen, from the bottom upward. It was a bridge, with a graceful suspended arch between two towers, each with a light that blipped on and off at the top. "That looks like the Golden Gate Bridge," I said.

"It is." Jonathan still stared intently at the screen, where a fiery glow of light appeared at the top. Slowly the light descended and I began to make out a round orange ball, sinking into the ocean just behind the bridge.

"Jonathan," I said, watching the golden sphere silently slide into the ocean, "Is that the sun setting?"

Jonathan frowned, and pulled his cap down over his forehead. "No, it's the moon setting." Without looking at me or changing his tone of voice, he said, "Now if it's raining outside, you can still have your moon group meeting."

"That's so cool. How in the world did you do it?"

"It's easy." He shrugged.

"I just love it!" I restrained my impulse to hug my grown-up twelve-year old. Instead I just grinned. "And now I have to go." As I lowered myself down through the closet, I don't think Jonathan saw the tears in my eyes.

Winter

Sunday Morning

I am tired and sleep late. Last night I gave a benefit performance at the Berkeley Peace Center. My son Jonathan's office was
right across the street.

I knew he was working intensely on a deadline for a new
program—"Star Trek: The Screen Saver." I wondered if he was
still working, and if he'd like to take a break and come see our
performance. But then I chastised myself. *He's probably under
too much pressure. I'm not sure he'd be interested. Besides, there's
no phone handy.*

It was a passing thought.

The performance included poetry and music by Asian
Americans, African Americans, and older women like me. I felt
uplifted by the solidarity and commitment to social justice in
our Berkeley community, and I went to bed exhausted but
exhilarated.

Jonathan moved out of our home a year ago. He bought

his own house at the age of nineteen, with two other friends and no financial help from us. He was especially proud of his garden and talked about it when he stopped by for supper last Tuesday. He spent the rest of the evening telling us about all the cheap restaurants in Berkeley where he could get a decent quick meal. "I'm getting tired of pizzas from Costco," he added.

As usual, he did not say much about himself except that he was working day and night with the "Star Trek" team of engineers at the computer company where he worked, Berkeley Systems, to meet their deadline. He seemed a bit tense, on edge, but nothing unusual. I was glad he stopped in for supper, because we rarely saw him these days.

During the night, I vaguely heard the answering machine drone on a couple of times, and I grew annoyed, thinking that some crank was probably making an obscene call.

In the morning, on my way downstairs to get tea, I check the machine: "This is the Berkeley police. Are you home? Please pick up the phone." And a second message: "This is the Berkeley police at your door. Please pick up the phone."

How irritating. Some kids amusing themselves with prank calls, I think.

I make morning tea and English muffins to have in bed with my husband Robin. A Sunday morning treat, until my friend Mayumi calls.

"Edie, some officers came to my door this morning asking

for you. You'd better check on your children."

"What do you mean? They're home in bed right now..." Suddenly my hands feel cold, and I start shaking all over. "Oh my God, Mayumi, Jonathan! I'll call you right back."

Mayumi's words spin through my head, making me dizzy. I feel like a block of ice, unable to move, unable to pick up the telephone. I must be nuts to call at this hour on a Sunday morning! I'm being a worrywart. But I have to call. I can hardly dial Jonathan's house; my hand shakes so violently.

"Chris," I say, "This is Edie. We got some weird calls on our answering machine last night. Is Jonathan okay?"

A pause. A horrible cold sweat drips down my back and chest. I know something terrible has happened.

"No. He's not. He killed himself last night."

Sandwich Hug

At a great distance, as if burning through a thick gray fog, I hear a low growling moan. I cannot move. I am floating up on top of the room, looking down at a woman with her mouth open, in her bathrobe. Suddenly a shattering, high-pitched wail starts me shaking all over.

What the hell is that ghastly noise? I wonder, and then I realize. *Oh my God, it's me.* It must be me. I clamp my hand over my mouth. The children are still asleep, and I don't want to scare them.

It can't be true; it just can't be true. I wrap my arms around myself, trying to stop the shaking. He's lying—I'll call back, that's what I'll do.

"Robin, Robin!" I hear the screaming again, "Helllllllllllp. Jonathan's dead. Our baby's dead..."

I grip the wooden banister tightly, one step at a time. One more step, I tell myself, then the hall, open the door...The stairwell is utterly silent. I hear a strange calm voice coming from nowhere. *It will be worse for Robin. You have to help him. All the love he gave Jonathan. They're so much alike. Robin lost his own Dad. He was only eight. And now his son... It will be worse for him.*

My throat closes and I can hardly breathe. An iron clamp around my chest squeezes all the blood out of me. I have become transparent and cannot feel my body at all. Only a huge hole and an outpouring from the center of myself, like a silver river.

I open the door to the hallway. Robin stares at me, his mouth open, his fluff of graying red hair still rumpled with sleep. His long blue and white kimono bathrobe is inside out, and his knobby knees stick out. He looks pale green. I can only squeak out a whimper: "Jonathan's dead."

"WHAT? That can't be! It's impossible!" Robin's face flushes bright red. He hunches over, sobbing. I shake uncontrollably in his arms, trying to say something coherent.

Benji, our younger son, bangs his bedroom door open, and then our daughter Keshi does the same, and they both run over to us, still in their pajamas.

"What? What is it?"

Robin and I stand on either side of them, put our arms around them both, and hug them tightly into the middle.

On Sunday mornings, already seemingly a lifetime ago, we

used to scrunch them up between us in the warmth of a leisurely sun-filled moment.

Laughing together with them, we would say: "Let's have a sandwich hug! You're the peanut butter and jam, and we're the bread!"

Want a Photo?

I have no idea where we are. Somewhere down under the freeway near the Oakland Port. Heavy December rains pound down onto the rooftop of our twenty-year-old Peugeot. Water drips down my neck through the old sliding roof, which doesn't work any more. God, it's so damned cold. I wish the heater worked.

The windshield wipers swipe furiously, making a horrid slapping sound, and dimly lit, the dark streets seem ominous in their emptiness. I feel an urge to scream and put my hand over my mouth. "Where in the world are we going? We must be lost."

Robin answers softly, "I've got a map. They said it was almost at the docks." He doesn't even look at the map.

I guess he's got the information in his head—thank God he's so good at directions.

We pull into a large empty parking lot. No street lights at all, only one huge, square, concrete building with a single light bulb over a door in the far corner.

"Are you sure this is it?" I am shaking and chilled to the bone. And now the rain pours harder than ever. My umbrella blows open and is useless.

"Let's go back. Can't we do this by phone?"

Robin takes my hand. His is sweaty but firm as we walk into a large, cavernous warehouse. "They said second floor. There's no elevator."

He walks ahead of me up a narrow concrete stairway. I can't see a thing and hold tight to the banister and to Robin. A small sign hangs at the top of the dark stairwell next to a door with a bare light bulb over it. The sign reads "Coroner's Office."

The officer pulls a small Polaroid photo out of a red file labeled HARTSHORNE, SUICIDE.

"Is this your son?" The officer holds up the photo. "We need your signatures, social security numbers, and affidavit. Is this your son?" He asks again, and looks sideways past Robin's ear. He is the only person on duty at this hour. He gets out two more photos.

I grab Robin's arm. I feel as if I will fall over any minute, and I try not to look, but then I whisper, "Let me see."

Jonathan lies face up on his bed, his hands outstretched over his head, fists clenched, with a torn black garbage bag over his head. His mouth is open. I look away and finally reply. "Yes. That's Jonathan. I want him back. At least let us see him and take him home."

"Regulations, ma'am. He's in the morgue. Have to sign the papers first. Do you want to take the photo with you?"

Answering Machine Madness

I'm going crazy, and I'm ashamed to tell anyone! It must be the middle of the night. Robin and the kids are sound asleep. Thank God, they can sleep. I've been lying awake trying not to scream since 1 A.M.

I sneak downstairs so I can call Jonathan at his work extension. I listen to his live voice again: *"Hello, Jonathan Hartshorne speaking. Leave a message and I'll call back as soon as possible. If you need immediate assistance press zero."*

Hearing him sounding so competent, I sob into the phone and talk to him. "Jonathan why did you do it? Why did you leave us? I love you. I miss you. Please call me back."

Then I cry alone in the cold living room, and look at photos of him when he was a baby, until I can't cry anymore. It is dark and cold, but the moon is still up. Morning will not come for a long time.

Tomorrow I will call Wes, the president of Jonathan's company, and I'll ask if he can leave Jonathan's message on the answering machine just a little longer.

I must be out of my mind. I wonder if they're listening to my messages. Maybe I should try writing letters to Jonathan instead. I can't go on like this.

A Cord of Wood and
a Black Frame

The phone's been ringing since 6 A.M. yesterday. Seems as if everyone knows. Don't ask me how. I've made no calls until now, but I suddenly want to speak to my twin brother Hal in Boston. It's 4 A.M. here, and I figure he'll just be getting ready to go to work—it's 7 A.M. there.

His wife, Diana, also a doctor, picks up the phone. We've recently had a family tiff, and I'm not expecting her to answer. I haven't the slightest idea what to say. Yet out of nowhere, I blurt, in a voice I hardly recognize, "Diana. I have something terrible to say. But first, I want to ask you to forgive me. Please forgive me for whatever pain I caused you. Forgive me—please. Jonathan's dead. He killed himself last night."

Silence.

"Ohmygod! Of course I forgive you. It's nothing compared to this. Nothing. Hal's in LA giving a paper, but I'll call him right away."

Ten years ago, Hal and Diana's four-year-old daughter

Rebecca died as they watched over her helplessly in Children's Hospital. Now we are twins again. I hang up the phone wanting my brother.

Hal arrives from LA in four hours. He folds me into his muscular hug, his hair slicked down and face unshaven. He holds me for a long time without speaking. After lunch, my brother goes out and buys a cord of wood, stacks it under the house, buys a black frame for Jonathan's photo, and makes all the arrangements at the funeral home. Finally, he looks me in the eye and says, "It gets worse later."

I don't believe him.

On A Mission
To Save Your Screen

The silence in this empty house rings in my ears. Drives me crazy. I go into the study, sit down at my desk, take out my journal, and start writing:

Dear Jonathan,

I decided to write you a letter today instead of calling you up at Berkeley Systems. You've been dead for three days. I'm here all by myself in the house. Benji and Keshi went back to school today for the first time since you left. I don't know how they can stand it. I can't go on living without you. Robin and your Uncle Hal have gone out for a hike in Tilden Park. So I'm alone—just with you.

I put my favorite photos of you all around my desk. Look how adorable you are—just three years old, busy trying to unscrew my ear with your new tool kit. I can hardly bear to look and remember.

And here you are just recently, in my favorite photo that your Uncle Hal put into a black frame. You're grinning and holding up the Berkeley Systems t-shirt. I don't even know why you won it — for outstanding contribution in your first year with the company? For tech support? For programming? This photo must have been taken just a few weeks ago. You're smiling shyly, as you show your prize with a print of those hilarious little toasters with wings flying through a sky filled with plump clouds. That's my favorite screen saver.

Oh dear Jonathan, I hardly know a thing about your work. You always seemed annoyed when I asked. You were so private and I didn't want to interfere. I thought you were just spreading your wings, becoming independent. Maybe I was wrong. And now it's too late. I'll never know. I was so proud of you, working as a computer engineer. I remember you telling me you'd gotten an A+ evaluation at the end of your first year. You seemed so confident and pleased with yourself. I just can't believe you really wanted to die. I wonder if the coroner's report is wrong.

Just last Saturday night, all alone in your bedroom, when you looked down at your lifeless body did you say, "Oh shit! What the fuck did I do that for?" Did you hear us wailing in disbelief when we found out the next morning? Don't you want to tell us that your death was a stupid mistake?

Oh, dear Jonathan — why in the world did you do such a stupid thing? I am so mad I could kill you myself! I want to howl until I'm hoarse and tear apart the walls of this house and run *naked into the street. Why did you leave us? I want you back!*

   I can't go on writing. I'm crying into my journal.

   Bye. I love you.

   — Your mad, sad, confused Mom

Bow Legged and Wearing Tevas

I have been sitting alone, looking out the kitchen window, up past the front garden, at the street for an hour. Robin is reading a 1743 edition of Euclid in the living room. My brother Hal is out buying groceries. I'm confused about what's best for the kids. Would it be better to let them skip school, or for them to keep on with their regular routines? The teachers say either way is okay. Today they both wanted to stay home, so we said fine. My brain doesn't seem to work anymore. I cannot make any decisions.

I'm sure the woman I spoke to on the phone at the mortuary's office said the men would arrive at nine sharp, and here it is almost ten. Where in the world are they? I see a long black van backing into the driveway. No windows. Four men in suits get out and two open the back doors of the van. They begin pulling something out.

Two fat gray men in front and two behind come step by step down the steep front pathway from the street, past the straggly rose bushes and brown remnants of untrimmed irises. A large wooden box lurches between them.

I jump up to see better and knock over the teapot, which shatters on the floor. "Oh my God he's coming back. Jonathan's coming home. Robin, they're here! Benji, Keshi—come downstairs. Jonathan's back. I open the front door and stare.

"Where do you want him, Ma'am?" The man looks past me avoiding my eyes.

"In here, in here, under the big window." I gesture.

"Do you want just the top half open, or the whole lid off?"

"I want to see all of him." I wait while they take off the two parts of the lid. Finally, they leave. Robin and the kids still haven't come down stairs.

"Is it really you, Jonathan?"

He looks so big in that box. He seems asleep. His hair is clean and brushed, his cheeks sunken, his skin a pallid strange color, and his lips are painted a weird purplish color. He wears his Tevas and his feet point out.

"Must be why you have that funny bow-legged walk just like Robin, and your arches are so high. Your hair looks soft and fluffy. Can I touch it?" And then, "I hope the kids don't hear me talking to you."

Cold Like Cement

That night I dream I am back in Mexico, working in the small Indian village where I lived when I was Jonathan's age. I see my friend Doña Juana and she carries her dead baby in a bag over her shoulder. The bag bears a dark, dry brown stain.

"She is dead, can't you see?" I say to Doña Juana. *"Nothing will bring her back to life. She is hard and cold like my son Jonathan."*

I wake up with a start and sneak downstairs to look at Jonathan again. I kiss him on his cold forehead. Cold like cement. This is not human flesh, this hard pallid cheek.

Even though everyone else is asleep, I look all around the living room, just to be sure no one watches. Then I take out my scissors and snip a big shock of hair—off the side of Jonathan's head, rather than the front, so it won't be too noticeable. I open the gold locket with pearls around it that my Quaker grandmother Bema gave me, tuck in the hair, and click it shut.

I sit and stare at him until the moon rides low on the horizon.

Sort of Like Thanksgiving

Despite our concerns for her recent arterial by-pass, my mom—a feisty eighty-two-year-old amputee—insists on flying 3,000 miles from Boston to be with us. I hug her at the doorway without saying a word. Her crutches clatter to the ground. She seems smaller and bonier than the last time I saw her.

My voice comes out in a squeak. "Thank thee for coming, Ma." I feel like a little girl again, and I greet her in the familiar Quaker words of my childhood. Speaking in this intimate second person to my mom gives me the feeling of being safe, of belonging. For a moment I feel held by the long ago wisdom of the white haired Elders in the Quaker Meeting House in Cambridge.

"I'm glad to see thee, dear." She wears the same tweed skirt and old ratty red down ski parka she has had for twenty years. Her blue eyes seem grayer than I remember, and when she holds on to me and I can feel all her ribs. Yet her words are like a blessing in the midst of chaos.

My other brother, his wife, and four of my seven East Coast nieces and nephews managed to get a flight with my mom. They all arrive from the airport at once, sopping wet. Robin and I stand at the doorway together, greeting my family, taking their umbrellas and dripping overcoats.

Robin takes everyone into the kitchen, puts on the tea, and we all scrunch around the little kitchen table. For a split second, I feel safe, protected by the kindness of my family arriving so unexpectedly.

Robin asks me to come into the living room for a minute with him. He hugs me and starts crying again.

"It feels like a party. Sort of like Thanksgiving. Then I remember why everyone's here…"

"Look What I Can Do Now!"

The full moon blazes and wakes me again. Everyone else is asleep and I'm sweating, roasting hot. I can't stay in bed one more second. I sneak downstairs into the study and don't look into the living room. I want to be with Jonathan, to stroke his hair, to watch him sleep the way I used to when he was a baby, yet I can't bear to look. I've got to write or I'll go nuts. I don't want to forget a single moment of what happened yesterday at Jonathan's memorial service.

All our friends and family crammed into the living room to say goodbye. Jonathan lay in his coffin underneath the plate glass window overlooking the San Francisco Bay. We put flowers all over his body, and around the coffin along with the model trucks he made when he was little, photos, and all the letters that have been stuffing our mailbox.

Mom sat next to me, nesting my sorrow in her silence. I clutched her warm hand with its rumpled blue veins protruding. Mine was limp and cold. As I wept, she comforted me, the broken bird.

We opened the service with music. I rang the large black Japanese temple bell Mom had given me for my fiftieth birthday. It had belonged to her mother, and the deep tones of the bell spiraled around the room. After a moment, they calmed me enough to welcome everyone.

Robin, Benji, Keshi and I all played music. It seemed easier than trying to say something.

Robin's haunting bamboo *shakuhachi* piece, "Tamuke," traditionally played for funerals in Japan, invited Jonathan's spirit to enter the room and join us. I remembered listening to Robin play this piece for a dear friend when we lived in Kyoto years ago. Like a loon calling her lost mate across a lake, the lament silenced our living room and sang from Robin's soul.

Keshi played a violin duet with her best friend. She wore a black dress and her dark hair hung over one eye. Benji played *The Elegy* on his cello—a slow melancholic piece written by Fauré for his young love who had died. He played it so slowly I thought it would never end. Then he sank into my lap, buried his head, and cried.

Everyone told stories about Jonathan.

"He was one of the most brilliant kids I ever met," his boss Wes said. "At first I wasn't sure if I should hire him—only eighteen and just out of high school! But he seemed so bright and eager, I gave him a job answering the phones, providing tech support. One day I noticed him helping frustrated customers on the phone, his head slightly to the side, holding the phone between his ear and shoulder talking politely, staring into space while obviously concentrating on the problem. Simultaneously, he was writing new programs. He really seemed to be enjoying himself. I promoted him to engineer status after a year.

"He also had a great sense of humor. A couple of weeks ago we came into the office and there was a can of tuna fish sitting on every desk. We were sure it was Jonathan."

The ripple of laughter helped me take a deep breath. If he was joking around, he wouldn't have killed himself on purpose, would he?

My friend Mayumi came with Pamela, Kaz and all of our Buddhist Artists for Peace group. Jonathan had often helped us format flyers and performance publicity. Mayumi spoke of the golden Jizo statue standing so serenely next to Jonathan's coffin. A Japanese friend gave us this beautiful golden Buddha figure right after Jonathan's birth in Kyoto, twenty years ago.

I drifted back to the day before Jonathan's birth. The cherry blossoms were in full bloom, and with the gentle spring rain, they fell like pink clouds all over the temple pathways and streams of Kyoto. Robin and I walked in the Heian Shrine, almost the only visitors in a place famous for its weeping cherry trees. The blossoms brushed against our cheeks, and Robin held my hand as we walked over the stepping-stones of the pond, lined with broad sweeps of purple iris in full bloom. Silently, we watched petals drift down and float across the pond. I prayed to Jizo, *Help me give birth to a healthy baby. I know I am ready.*

Mayumi interrupted my reverie, reminding us that Jizo is the guardian of children and of travelers in Japan. Just the guide Jonathan now needs, I thought. Is he a little baby soul now? Or is he himself, full grown? My thoughts pelted me, making it difficult to hear what anyone said.

Jonathan seemed so close. The cousins laughed and cried simultaneously, remembering summer holidays when we all visited together and they piled like puppies in the middle of our living room floor. Lisa told how they always counted on Jonathan to rescue them in the sailboats, to make it back home against the outgoing tide. One night, at our summer home near Boston, the cousins got Jonathan drunk at a beach party barbecue. The next day, Lisa said, "Hey Jonathan, do you remember when you climbed the windmill last night?"

"Come on! Did I really?"

Tears poured down Lisa's face as she recounted their teasing. Lisa was closest to Jonathan and always joked with him.

Like the others, she respected him and was in awe of his intelligence. He solved their problems and fixed things. As Lisa spoke, a bolt of lightning suddenly lit up the huge picture window and the San Francisco Bay beyond.

In high school, Jonathan spent weeks constructing a gigantic Tesla coil, large enough to send a twelve-inch spark. Now he's up there tossing lightning bolts across the sky.

I sensed his soul so young and new spinning through the firmament—a comet blazing with the lightning and rollicking thunder of the electrical storms we'd been having.

Jonathan, what are you doing up there? Are you sending us jokes from the next century, reminding us of our limited vision?

I could almost hear him laugh aloud. "You think I played tricks then?" he says. "Look what I can do now."

Our First Family Home

Dear Jonathan,

At your memorial service, you were so close I couldn't tell if you were still here or if you were being born again. Time is dissolving. It seems only a moment ago when we were on our way to Kyoto with you in my womb. We got bumped onto JAL first class because my belly was so big.

I had never been to Japan before, but when Robin described the beauty of quiet temples and gardens in Kyoto, the silence of mountainside walks on the Eastern side of the city, I thought to myself: What a beautiful place for you to be born. I agreed to go despite my fears about giving birth in a city where I knew no one and didn't speak the language.

I'm sure I never told you how disappointed I was when I trailed two steps behind Robin and his professor host, up the gray stairwell to our little one-room apartment in Kyoto University's Konoe Hall. Robin had been invited to the Mathematics Research

Institute, as a visiting professor, and I had imagined they would give us a lovely Japanese home.

Instead, the frosted windows in our gray concrete room prevented me from seeing even a tree or a bit of sky. I tried rubbing them with olive oil and then the room smelled. The noise from the trolleys just below our window was so loud that we couldn't talk when they rumbled by. I shut the door to the bathroom, sat on the toilet and cried. How could I bring you home to such a gloomy place?

The next day Dorothy called from the Aoibashi Family Clinic. Dorothy had heard of me from a social worker friend who lived in Boston. She was looking for an American-trained therapist to assist her in the clinic.

The moment I passed through the Japanese wooden gate to her garden, the clatter of the city fell away, as if I had entered the world of my fantasy. A serene, protected garden with pine, bamboo, and plum trees, carefully pruned azalea bushes, moss-covered rocks, and a stone fountain stood sentinel before me. At the end of the stepping-stone pathway, still gray with morning rain, welcoming wood and paper sliding shoji doors led to the Genkan entranceway.

The small clinic, wrapped in morning mist, enclosed the garden, and each room looked out onto a different view. I stood silently in the garden's serene embrace before entering the clinic. This would be our first family home.

When we returned to Berkeley, we missed Kyoto so much that we built a Japanese teahouse inside the garage. I emptied out all our stuff, boxes of used clothes, toys, old files and papers, and two cat boxes. You wanted to keep your old sled, but we took everything else to Goodwill.

So many things I never told you while you were alive. And now so much of your life comes back to me. Across the barrier of death, may I tell you of my unspoken loves and longings?

—Your drowning-in-memories Mom

A Dumpling Bun

Dear Jonathan,

The rain finally let up for a moment so the rest of the family all went out for a hike in Tilden Park. I'm looking at your baby pictures. So vividly, I remember that moment you transformed our lives, falling like a sapphire star into my heart. Dear Jonathan, imagine—I've been writing to you ever since you were born. I just found this song I wrote for you in my old Kyoto journal. You were four days old. Of course, I never would have shown it to you while you were alive. But now everything's different.

I call you by name—Jonathan. You are separate yet part of me. You drink my body. I paint your colors and sing with joy as I feel you kick and turn. Such a long awaiting for you my son, yet I've known you all along in your father.

We prepare for you with flowers and music. Amida Buddha with compassion guards the gateway by our bedside. Your father sings out his private soul on ancient bamboo reed, shakuhachi—

song of the "Bell Ringing in the Empty Sky." On the crest of rising pain and bliss, I tremble.

I burst aflame, no boundaries to my passion now. And cry with joy for this exquisite moment of communion with you, new moist and dappled love; with your father, guardian of my raw awakening. Eyes damp as forest moss he smiles, flaming above me his crown of red-gold hair. Can I ever love and be as consumed as at this very moment?

My milk white floodgates open, tingling with delight at your nuzzling insistence. So warm and succulent a peach boy! Oh, how could any mother resist so ripe and plump a dumpling bun to kiss and nibble as you squeak with joy, a damp and succulent aroma thick as mango juices just beneath your peach ripe thighs? I shall eat you up I love you so, my damask oyster, cool and slippery on my tongue. I am ablaze with love.

These memories fill me with your smells, the silkiness of your skin. As if it were only an instant ago I can feel you lying upon my breast, a sapphire soul looking right into my eyes, falling like a star into my heart.

Now this broken heart can barely go on beating. I can't look at these photos anymore. I'll write tomorrow.

—Your sad and tender Mom

Family Resemblance

It's already nine-thirty when I finally drag myself out of bed. Benji and four cousins meet in the kitchen dressed in jogging shorts and light rain parkas. Chris places his foot up on the counter, Nike running shoe perched on the chopping block. He folds over like a hairpin, lengthening his hamstrings. Ali stretches against the wall. She has been trying out for the All American Rowing team, and her calf muscles are large and well defined. Benji ran cross-country all fall with the high school team, and he seems pleased to take his cousins on a jogging tour of Berkeley.

"Wait 'til you see the view at the top of Grizzly," he says, lacing up muddy track shoes. The endless winter drizzle doesn't faze them in the slightest.

An hour later, they return red-cheeked and laughing, and drop their wet rain gear in the front hall.

"Man, that Marin Avenue is as steep as the headwall on Mt.

Washington," Chris says, still panting. When I see the bright flush on their faces, I feel that same glow of warmth and exhilaration, the pleasure of dripping with sweat, my heart beating, feeling so alive. For a moment, I am happy again.

Robin and I cook a huge breakfast of omelets, French toast and fruit, apple sausages and vegetable quiches for the vegetarians. Hal, Robin, Mom, and the rest of my family cram around the kitchen table. Keshi and Jonathan's favorite cousin, Lisa, sleep late.

Benji puts up a card table for his cousins and for an instant, it seems like vacation, when we all gather together at my grand parents' home for family reunions. The phone interrupts my memories.

"Edie this is Wes, would you and your family like to come down and visit Berkeley Systems and see Jonathan's office?"

At first I can't speak. But I know the cousins would get a kick out of seeing Jonathan's office, so we loan my mom a rain jacket to put over her no-longer waterproof red parka, and persuade her that it is too far to walk on crutches.

"We'll all switch off pushing thee in thy wheel chair," Benji says. We get out all the umbrellas we can find and parade down our street through the Solano tunnel, all the way to Jonathan's office. The cousins all have a familiar family look. Only Jonathan is missing.

Flying Toasters

Dear Jonathan,

Were you watching when our whole family went down to visit your office a few days ago? Your East Coast cousins were really impressed. Guess what? Wes gave me two boxes filled with screen-saver souvenirs. We opened them right up and all put on sweatshirts with little toasters flying above puffy white clouds, that signature piece of your company. Under them text read: The 52nd Squadron on a Mission to Save Your Screen. Eric, Andy, Uncle Hal, and Robin wore the neckties with miniature flying toasters. They almost looked like businessmen. Wes gave us several copies of Star Trek: The Screen Saver as well as lots of toaster buttons and inflatable blue flying toaster balloons. Right this minute there are four blue toasters flying all around our kitchen. Everyone asks what in the world they are doing up there.

Do you remember the very first time you took me to your office? On a Saturday, when no one was there? You had a huge ring of keys on your belt that clanged as you got off your red motorcycle to meet me in the parking lot. I bit my lips when I saw you wore Tevas and no helmet. You certainly were determined to do things your own way, weren't you? Maybe that's partly how you leaped over the usual professional stages to become a computer engineer. Dear Jonathan—I was so proud of you. Did you know it?

You started my tour at the reception desk, "Here's where Jan sits, and here are all the products we've already sent out." You loped down the hall too quickly for me to read the names. "Here's a New York Times article about us. Here's the accounting office, and the storeroom and over here is where our team's working on Star Trek: The Screen Saver.

Then you took me to the "Board Room," just beyond the huge fish tank in the lobby. Standing on Greek pillars surrounding a large oval table were toasters of every vintage: little square toasters with a black knob to push down; skinny toasters with slender sides that flapped open; toasters that had a red bell to sound an alert when the toast was cooked, and a large silver toaster with golden wings.

"That's the toaster we take to exhibits," you explained. "Wes asked me to take it on the plane when we go to Macworld Expo next summer. By the way, my program 'Gravity' is going to be on the exhibit screen at our booth."

You looked away with that shy embarrassed look. I restrained myself from jumping up and down and hugging you.

–Your Mom

White Crane Prayer

Two days ago, they came and took Jonathan away. I wanted him to stay one day longer. I begged them to come back tomorrow— "Just one more day with me? This is where he grew up," I argued.

Today I feel leaden, unable to move. So I sit in the living room for a while and do nothing. I am gazing out the living room window, imagining Jonathan lying below it, still in his coffin, when the doorbell rings. A man in a blue pin striped suit, necktie and black shoes asks me: "Are you Mrs. Hartshorne?" He hands me a heavy box wrapped in brown paper, turns away and mumbles "I'm sorry ma'am."

I take the box into the living room, tear off the brown paper, and stare at the gray steel lid. I cannot bear to open it. I break a fingernail prying open the lid. Shutting my eyes tight, I plunge in my hand, close my fingers into a fist around the soft powdery dust. It feels gritty. Finally, I open my eyes, look at my open palm and see tiny bits of white bone.

What happened to Jonathan's body? Did they slide it into a huge oven? I wish I could have seen. I wish we could have watched him go up in smoke on a funeral pyre. Instead, they bring us this cold steel box. Is that all that is left of my big tall son?

I wrap the box with a cloth of golden cranes, given to Jonathan when he was born in Japan. I remember a Japanese prayer offered to the white crane, omen of long life and good fortune:

Oh great bird, great bird, wrap my child in your wings.

I place the box carefully in the *tokonoma* altar place of our Japanese teahouse. I light a candle, ring the black Japanese temple bell and pray for Jonathan's soul. I pray also that I might be able to sleep tonight.

As I am falling asleep Jonathan startles me and I bolt up, wide awake. The great heat that pours through my body is as brilliant as the lightning that set our living room ablaze with light four days ago. It starts in my feet, and pulses upward, filling my legs, thighs, belly, and torso until finally it pours into my head. I have the impression I am radiating intense yellow and white light. I am wide-awake, not dreaming, yet I cannot move, and the heat does not burn me.

I can feel him in my body, as surely as during those nine months I carried him in my womb. The huge darkened sky fills with his face, and he smiles as he says to me, *I'm okay. I love you. And I know you loved me.*

I do not wake up Robin. He has enough trouble sleeping. Besides—what can I tell him? I lie awake for a long time wondering. Jonathan, are you trying to tell me your death was an accident, a horrible mistake?

Surprise Visit

This morning Jonathan's best friend, Ben Resner, called and asked if he could stop by for a visit. We sat in the kitchen, watching the rain fall on the front garden while we chatted.

"I loved Jonathan," Ben said. "He was an amazing guy."

Ben also told me how he lived through the suicide of his own father, of how this experience had sensitized him to depression, and of his doubts about Jonathan's death.

"Ben, I'm so grateful you came by. That question's gnawing on me. Also, I just found out there was an error in the police report. They said there were CO_2 cartridges lying on the floor in Jonathan's room. Now we have found out from one of his roommates that they were nitrous oxide cartridges taken from whipped cream canisters. I wonder what other errors the police made."

"Nitrous!" Ben interrupted. "Yeah, we used to call inhaling nitrous a "power break". Nice safe high, and you can go right back to what you were doing."

"But Ben, Jonathan wasn't into drugs, at least I don't *think* he was. How did he know about nitrous?"

"How did he know about sex?" Ben laughed.

Ben then read me this excerpt from his journal, written two days after Jonathan died:

I am sitting here at work, writing. Not because I'm bored or frustrated or seriously considering an immediate career change, but because Jonathan Hartshorne apparently committed suicide yesterday. I say apparently because the circumstances just don't add up. I have no memories of him reaching out and me pushing back. He was a respected member of the programmers and Berkeley Systems culture in general, and he was aware of this. Yes, he was young and talented and had never been to college, but he was in control of this. Thinking back, I can't locate any incident where I should have thought "hmmm," or been more responsive.

In many ways, it's difficult to sort out emotions because the exact nature of his death is still so unsettled. It's ghoulish to seek out details, but there are too many open questions. I can't help but suspect it was an accident.

I'm surprised at how not-guilty I feel. I almost feel obligated to assume some sort of minimal guilt. I said to Jonathan about two weeks ago that I had probably spent more time in his proximity than with all other people combined, because we had spent so much time sitting next to each other during the course of Star

Trek *development. It's no secret that I deeply pride myself on my ability to not only be receptive when other people reach out for help, but to create an environment where people can approach me with their problems, when they might have otherwise kept them bottled inside.*

Now I sit alone in the teahouse, meditating and wondering what in the world to do with this information. I don't know what to think anymore.

Beyond The Bamboo Garden Wall

Dear Jonathan,

Your friend Ben Resner stopped by yesterday. I'm totally confused. The Police say your death was suicide. Ben disagrees. I wish you would come again and speak to me.

All I know is that I want to be close to you, so I put your ashes in the teahouse. I figure you'll feel right at home there. I know it sounds weird, but I'm swimming in memories. I can hardly tell if I'm awake or dreaming. It's comforting to share them with you. I want to tell you about when we brought you home from the hospital in Kyoto. The nurses at Baptist Byoin Hospital hardly let me get a wink of sleep, they were so curious and eager to see an American baby and practice their English.

Dorothy had invited me to be Acting Director of the Aoibashi Family Clinic while she was away, so three days after your birth we moved in. My Japanese colleagues came into the kitchen of the clinic one morning to admire you, and everyone laughed when Robin gave you your first bath in a little washtub on the kitchen table. You floated calmly in the warm water while Robin held your head and pinched your ears shut so as not to get water in them.

Our friends asked, "Is this what American husbands do?"

How long ago I stood in the small Japanese garden and heard the swift uplifting rush of wings beyond the bamboo garden wall. Sliding aside the wooden gate, we stepped outside into the narrow Kyoto streets for our first walk with you to the local temple, to celebrate Children's Day. Our neighbors paused and peeked into the quilted baby wrap, admiring your unfamiliar features.

"Look—he's completely bald."

Other parents with newborns and infants smiled at us, bowed in polite Japanese fashion as they strolled down the tree-lined corridor to the shrine. Several baby girls had on long kimonos to celebrate the special day designated to bless and give thanks for children. Their bursts of jet-black hair stuck straight up. Shining, their red cheeks look ripe enough to pluck. We chatted and laughed and admired their beauty. You astonished the other parents. "What a large head he has! Surely he will be a genius, just like Robin," they commented, as they crowded around. When we walked under the great orange Torii gate leading up to the Shinto shrine, I knew we had passed through another kind of gateway.

We strolled by a small Jizo statue—a simple round stone, partly covered with the red bib-like cloth so common in Kyoto— placed in a modest wooden shrine. I might not have noticed it, but on that day I thought Jizo watched over us, and I felt well protected.

Now I wish we had stayed in Kyoto.

—Your dreaming Mom

Sail Away for a Year and a Day

Before supper we gather in the living room for our weekly family meeting with our teenage kids. Keshi curls into the far corner of the sofa with her math homework. A small brown bear nestles in her lap. The silence is broken only by the creek of my mom's old mahogany rocking chair, a wedding gift reminding me of when I was a child. Benji looks at the floor while pushing the chair back and forth, his long legs askew.

"I know you kids don't really like family meetings, but I think it's important" I say.

"How was school today?" Robin tries to help, looking at Benji.

"What are we having for supper?" Keshi peers over her math book.

"Stir-fried rice, chicken and broccoli." Stir-fried rice is Keshi's favorite. Maybe it will offset the broccoli. The creaking irritates my nerves. Benji says nothing.

"Did you think about Jonathan today?" I ask wishing I hadn't.

Silence.

Finally, "Haven't we talked about Jonathan enough?" Benji blurts. "I don't want any more family meetings. I wish you'd stop asking me. Let's make supper." He gets up and goes into the kitchen.

"OK. Meeting adjourned." Robin pushes back his chair and follows Benji. Keshi picks up her homework and sits down at the kitchen table. Robin chops the broccoli and Benji sets the dishes on four tablemats around Keshi's homework.

Benji opens the oven door to see if the chicken's done. "Smells good. Stuffed chicken. My favorite!" He takes a big whiff and smiles.

Dinner is ready. We hold hands Quaker style in silence. The kitchen table is just big enough for all four of us, a big bowl of stir-fried rice, the roast chicken and broccoli.

"Delicious" Benji says. "Hey Keshi, would you get some water?"

"I'm eating." She doesn't look up.

" You haven't done a *thing* to help."

Keshi starts crying and runs out of the room, slamming the door.

We three stop eating.

"I'm going up to her bedroom." I push my chair back and

rush up the stairs two steps at a time. Robin and then Benji follow.

I open Keshi's door. She's not there. Oh my God. I look to see if the window is open. Then I look under the bed. From the closet I hear a muffled "uhh uhh uhh" like a small animal squeaking. I open the door and see nothing in the darkness. Then under a blanket in the corner I make out a round hump and hear sobbing. I climb right into the closet under Keshi's clothes, pull off the blanket and scrunch myself down. I bundle Keshi onto my lap, hugging her to my chest.

"Remember the *Runaway Bunny*, that book we used to read when you were little?" I ask. "If you run away, I'll run away after you. If you sail away, I'll sail away with you. If you fly to the highest mountain, I'll fly up after you."

Robin pushes his way in under skirts and blue jeans. "If you swim across the ocean I'll swim along with you."

Benji folds himself in too. "If you ride your bike down Solano Ave. I'll ride along right after you."

We huddle together in silence.

The closet becomes stuffy and hot. Keshi is no longer crying.

Finally she speaks. "Let's go downstairs and finish that yummy fried rice. I bet it's still hot."

"Great idea," Benji backs out of the closet.

After the children are in bed, Robin and I and sit close

together on the sofa, looking out at the distant shining lights of San Francisco.

"Maybe we *are* talking too much about Jonathan. I've been trying not to cry while the kids are around, but I'm thinking even family meetings aren't useful. *I'm* the one who wants to talk." I confess to Robin.

"The kids need to get back into school and their normal routines. Let's plan to chat in the evenings," Robin says.

"I know just how Keshi feels. *I* wish I could sail away for a year and a day in a beautiful pea green boat, myself!

"When I sail back home again, maybe this will all just be a bad dream." I snuggle down deeper into the sofa.

A Bright Quirky Kid

Jonathan has been dead for eleven days, and Benji and Keshi are back at school. Robin is preparing his exams, and his last math classes on space curves in characteristic p. I am amazed that he is able to teach. He says he prepares his lectures as he bikes to school. It looks like rain today and I wonder if he will be safe biking home this afternoon. Maybe I should call him and tell him I will pick him up and put his bike in the trunk of our car.

I can't believe how much love still pours into our house. Friends come by every day, bringing food, poems, and memories of Jonathan, small snapshots from our shared past. Their love and generosity keeps me afloat. A poem snippet from Naomi Shihab Nye drifts into my mind:

Before you know what kindness really is
you must lose things,
feel the future dissolve in a moment

like salt in a weakened broth.
What you held in your hand,
what you counted and carefully saved,
all this must go so you know
how desolate the landscape can be
between the regions of kindness.

The desolation in my life is being softened by kindness from so many friends. Earlier today, Kay brought me a big pot of chicken soup. We reminisced while we drank tea in the kitchen. She recalled Jonathan at four years old. We had gone to Kay's house for dinner, and Kay had asked her son, seven-year-old Matthew, to produce his fire engine and the ambulance with a siren, because little Jonathan was coming to play. Soon after we arrived, Jonathan sat down amidst the trucks and wired the red light and alarm circuit on his Science and Circuits kit. "Watch this!" he said to Matthew. "Now the buzzer will ring and the red light will flash!" He closed the circuit and looked up with a grin.

"That was the end of playing with the fire trucks," Kay laughed. "He was so brilliant."

Tears streamed down my cheeks, but I could not help laughing as I remembered the circuits, radios, clocks, and eventually computers that Jonathan disassembled and reassembled, always curious to know what secrets they held.

"That's exactly how he was in kindergarten," I said. "One day, when I came to pick him up, he wasn't out playing on the jungle gym. The teacher explained that he had refused to come out for recess, so I found him in the classroom. He was sitting on the floor, legs wide apart, leaning over a plastic number 1 on the rug. At least thirty zeros followed the number, so they covered the entire distance from wall to wall.

"In Kinder Gym that same afternoon, the teacher attached a halter with a rope and pulley on Jonathan, so he wouldn't bounce off the trampoline and hurt himself. Jumping up to the sky he chattered away, merry as a sparrow. I can hear him so clearly: 'And that is the pulley. And that is the rope that holds me. And that is the rope that goes through the pulley. And that is the rope you are pulling...'"

"'Little Professor,' the instructor named him." We both laughed.

"I *did* worry a lot about him, Kay. He was so stubborn and unusual. But I never imagined this could happen to him."

Kay hugged me. "I'll go warm up the soup," she said. "You did everything you could for him. He was a bright, quirky kid. I don't believe he intended to die. I think it was an accident."

Waltz of the Flowers

Jonathan has been dead for two weeks. It seems like two years. Each morning when I try to meditate in the teahouse, I light a candle for him. Mostly I just cry. It's a relief that the kids still have school. What in the world will we do during the holidays? So called "Holy Days." Holy Hell Days—that's what they'll be. I have to control myself.

A friend, trying to comfort me, says, "One day your son will become a pearl."

I scream at her, "I don't want a pearl! I want my son back!"

Christmas is just a week away. At least we are trying to keep on with the kids' programs. So we decide to go all together to the Christmas performance of the Oakland Youth Orchestra, where Benji is first cellist. Robin and I are pleased that he wanted to perform despite Jonathan's death. Though Robin and I can still barely drag ourselves out of bed in the morning, Benji and Keshi seem to be doing okay in school. I worry that we're not giving them the attention they need.

At the Masonic Temple auditorium, I bend down as if to read the program, so the parent across the table will not notice the tears rolling down my cheeks. Robin looks wonderful in his suit. A little too tight now, but he left the pants button open under his belt. He wears his bird's nest hairdo and looks just like Einstein, with his graying mustache and long hair fluffed out.

The other day, Keshi gave him a postcard with a picture of Einstein reading. She wrote: "I never thought I'd love a Mathematician, but I do." Our children sustain us in ordinary moments.

On stage, the kids are tuning their instruments. Teenagers of all sizes and colors, dressed in formal black attire, fill the stage. They look grown up. Benji is chatting with his stand-mate, a beautiful Chinese girl with long black hair. He looks relaxed, and laughs as he leans down to fine-tune the A string. I am glad he can forget for a moment.

I drift into reverie, away from the concert hall: I have been unable to cook, cannot bear to go out. Christmas shopping seems obscene. Mindless consumption. To hide what suffering? I wonder—is there anyone else whose great pile of Christmas gifts obscures private sorrow?

Christmas carols spin through my mind. Those I used to love now taunt me: Sleep in heavenly peace. I burst into tears. Where is he? Sleeping in heaven? Or drifting, stunned, lost in

Bardo? What did I do wrong? Was I a terrible Mom?

Well-meaning acquaintances ask, "How are you?"

I feel like screaming, "Can't you see? I can hardly breathe! My skin is peeled off. My son is dead. I am congealing into a hard cold block of cement, like my dead son."

Then a voice inside calls me back to the present. *Here you are at a Christmas celebration, and your wonderful living son is sitting right there on stage, first chair, his golden hair shining under the stage lights. Look—a small white paper crane sits on his cello. He must have folded it while tuning up.*

The conductor walks on stage, and suddenly this collection of kids rises like a flock of birds soaring in unison up from the beach. Rumpled shirts of adolescence instantly disappear, and a moment later the hall begins to sway with Tchaikovsky's balmy phrases—*Waltz of the Flowers.*

I look up and see Benji waving his bow during the one-measure rest as if to say: "Come dance."

He dives back into the theme, prancing over the strings with such pleasure that I laugh out loud in spite of myself. I take Robin's hand and we waltz right up to the stage. In a moment, waltzing couples fill the entire hall. Benji is focused, concentrating, yet completely relaxed, enjoying the rhythm. He looks up from the music he has obviously memorized, gives us a great Benji grin, and goes on playing without missing a beat.

Sushi Spinning in Circles

January's here and the kids are back in school. Other parents take care of the carpools, but at least I can still make the kids' lunches. Robin has biked off to give a lecture. How in the world can he bike in all that traffic. Oh God, what if he gets hit? Just then I hear a thump on the ceiling, a muffled shuffling, water running upstairs. Must be the shower. No, the toilet.

The big black frying pan is starting to smoke right in front of me on the stove. There's nothing in it. What in the world was I trying to do? I turn off the stove and notice pancake mix, a milk carton, a large blue bowl and an egg on the counter. Oh yes, now I remember. Benji has a cross country competition today. How could I be so dumb? Yes that's it. I was making pancakes. He needs lots of carbs for the race. I mix everything together and stare as the batter bubbles. I ladle small amounts in the hot frying pan.

I decide to make Keshi a beautiful *obento,* a Japanese lunchbox, with bright colors and patterns to cheer myself up, with a little joke inside. There's got to be something I can do to keep from leaking tears all over the place. Into the little black lacquer box with delicate cherry blossoms painted on the side, I carefully arrange white rice, bright green beans, slices of Japanese omelet rolled like a crepe, nori—Japanese seaweed— and nestled in the middle of the box, a lovely plastic shrimp sushi. I pick it up, put it on the counter, and voilà! It runs around by itself on the table! Its tiny wheels and wind-up motor sit neatly concealed inside the shell. Watching that silly little shrimp spin around in circles on the counter top, I start laughing hysterically. I smell something burning. Oh shit! I forgot the pancakes. God. I can't even make my kids' lunches. I throw the first batch into the sink, wash the pan and start all over again.

Come on, Edie! I mumble sternly to myself in the kitchen, standing stupidly, my jaw hanging open—*who's the child in this family anyway?* Breathe, I tell myself. Just stop and breathe. Crying—breathing—meditation. I close my eyes. Stop. Imagine Benji rummaging around for his socks, Keshi putting together a chic outfit. What a darling child she is.

I had longed for a little girl but never could have imagined how Robin and I, in our fifties, might be given a daughter. We were close friends with Keshi's parents, Ethan and especially

Miyo, who was our teacher of Japanese classical music. While they were ill we agreed to adopt Keshi, and she came to live permanently with us when she was ten years old.

The carpool beeps loudly three times.

"The kids will be out in just a sec," I yell, opening the front door. I run back to the sink, douse my face in cold water, dry myself with a dishcloth and dab powder around my puffy eyes. I hope the kids don't notice. Benji leaps two steps at a time down the stairs, cello strapped to his back, grabs his lunch box and charges off. I quickly wrap up Keshi's *obento* in a *furoshiki*, (a Japanese scarf) just in time to hand it to her as she puts on her backpack, picks up her violin and follows Benji up the garden path.

The house reeks of silence. Maybe if I meditate I can get some perspective. I shuffle out to the teahouse, relieved to be in solitude. I sit down and ring the black temple bell. I've got to control myself at least until the kids leave for school. It isn't fair to them. I ring the bell, chant the heart sutra, and speak to Miyo: "Miyo—please come and guide me. I'm trying to keep my promise that I'll raise Keshi, but sometimes I'm not sure I have the strength to survive. I feel like putting a pillow over my head and never waking up again. But I promise you, no matter how horrible I feel, I'm not going to give up. Really I'm not. "Now Keshi's with us and Jonathan's with you. Please take care of him. Maybe you can find out what happened. Do you think he really meant to die? Would you still send Keshi to us now that I'm in a shambles?

"Miyo—please forgive me. I'm doing the best I can. I feel so vulnerable. How in the world does anyone ever learn to parent?"

Robin's Investigation

I finally have the energy to tell Robin about my doubts. Yesterday I showed him Ben's journal entry, told him about Kay's visit and both of their questioning whether Jonathan's death was really a suicide. Robin has been so distraught. It never occurred to him that the police may have misinformed the Coroner's Office, but finally he too wonders, and he has decided to do his own investigation.

He went over to Jonathan's house, looked around the garage and discovered that the day before Jonathan died, he had bought a lever holder, an R. Flasher light assembly and an economy mercury carburetor tuner for his motorcycle. Jonathan had worked for about two hours on his motorcycle that day. In his garage, Robin found the manual open to the page on setting up carburetor tuners, and he also found little plugs from his carburetor on the floor. "No one suicidal would repair his motorcycle the day of his death," Robin told me. "And two days before he died, he removed party decorations from Berkeley Systems. His colleagues said he was his usual pleasant, serious self."

Robin also discovered that the day before he died Jonathan visited a doctor seeking treatment for his acne.

"These look like the signs of any 20 year old looking forward to future events," Robin said. "I think there's a lot more to find out. I'm going to look into some of the medical literature and study about suicide. I'm determined to understand what happened, no matter what the final outcome."

I Know More About
Termites

Dear Jonathan,

I drove by your house today. I know it's a stupid thing to do. I can't even bear to park and peek in. I just snatch a furtive glance. I remember that afternoon Robin and I both held our tongues and said nothing when you dropped in and told us you were going to buy a house with your friends Rob and Jake.

"Buy a house? How in the world are you planning to finance that?" we wondered. Even three young computer wizards—how could you make the down payment? You knew that we couldn't help you.

In your typically independent and thorough way you looked at nineteen houses, inspected them from attic to cellar, learned all about loans, mortgages, dry rot and termites. Some time later you came for supper. You were wearing your standard outfit: Tevas, shorts with a vice grip hanging from the belt loop in case you needed to fix something, and a t-shirt with the Star Ship Enterprise on it.

You announced:

"I know more about termites now than I ever wanted to know! Our offer for the house just got accepted. I'm pretty sure escrow will go through. We'll move in a month!"

We were so proud of you! When the deal actually did go through we celebrated, and your older cousin Eric posted a note in the family newsletter: "Jonathan is the first one in the next generation to buy a house!"

Your colleagues at work kidded you when you all went out to get a beer. "Hey, here comes the kid! He's old enough to buy a house but not old enough to buy a beer!" All my love.

—Your Mom

Like a Virus

Jonathan has been dead for nine weeks. The children are in school, and I need time alone. So today, I'm having my own private retreat in my teahouse sanctuary. The rains have finally let up, and sunlight streams through the bamboo doors to make patterns on the straw *tatami* mats. They smell fresh. The room is completely empty except for my *zabuton* and *zafu* pillows and the temple bell. On one wall is a large six-panel Japanese screen with mountains in the distance, clouds speckled with golden light, and a small fishing boat in the foreground. Empty space. Just what I need.

I feel such relief out of the house, in a place where I needn't speak to a soul, needn't answer the phone and hear the endless questioning, "How are you? How are you, how *are* you?"

What would happen if I blurted out the truth?

"I'm horrible. I feel like screaming and raging. I'm angry with everyone. I almost blurt out blame at Robin, at Jonathan's friends and mostly at myself. I have to bite my tongue and choke on my own thoughts. Some friends have stopped calling. They don't want to hear. It might be catching, like a virus. Am I getting paranoid?"

These days I can hardly bear to be with anyone I don't know well. When I say to a small circle of women acquaintances, "Six weeks ago my son committed suicide," I can feel the gasp in the room, the rush of horror jolting each woman for an instant. The discomfort is palpable.

I avert my eyes. I can't bear for anyone to know what I'm thinking: *Don't worry, I won't ask you to confront this unthinkable, this most ghastly nightmare of every mother. I pray you will never bolt upright to hear a voice on the phone that turns your blood to ice.*

I'm still not convinced that Jonathan killed himself. Yet I keep saying the words, as if by speaking them aloud I can go back in time, rewrite the whole story.

Why does everyone keep asking, "How did it happen? Was he depressed? Did you have any indication?" I wonder if they're hoping to hear, "Yes, he was depressed," so they can think, "This won't possibly happen to me, because *my* child was never that introverted, never that eccentric."

They want protection from that bolt of lightning that strikes suddenly and sizzles the heart, strips off flesh in an instant. They don't want to be left in this hell, hanging on a meat hook, raw nerves exposed to any passerby—as I am.

That's why I hide in my teahouse sanctuary.

Shedding the Garments of her Skin

Almost every morning, I still wake up in turmoil at five o'clock, unable to sleep, remembering Jonathan's death. God, he's been dead for almost three months! When will this ever end? It's not even light yet, and I feel like calling my mother in Cambridge. I know she'll be awake by now.

I wonder if Keshi wishes she could call *her* mom. How in the world can I ever fill that void for her? I want to help her with her suffering, but here I am again roiling in waves of my own. Now I am Keshi's mom, and yet I am swimming in the waters of mother-longing, dead and alive: Miyo, Keshi, me and my mom—I hardly know where to turn.

So I give in, slip out of bed so as not to wake Robin, turn on the lights, sneak downstairs and make a cup of tea. Feeling like a little girl again, I phone my mom.

"It's snowing here," she says. "What's it like there?"

"The iris are just poking their shoots up. They're telling my garden it's time to wake up!"

My mom must be looking out her kitchen window as she speaks to me. "There's a squirrel trying to crawl down into the bird feeder! He's chattering and squeaking, slipping on the snow. He's so angry that he can't get at the birdseed! Oh, he is so funny!"

Three thousand miles apart, we laugh together. Just for a moment, my pain vanishes. How grateful I am that I can rest for an instant, as if I could lean up against her old sagging breast.

Spring

Laughing Gas

My friend Kay stops by again today. I get some tea and we sit down on the sofa.

"You know, Kay, when the police first told me Jonathan's death was suicide, I felt my whole body screaming. And then friends started calling from around the country saying they had heard of teenagers accidentally suffocating while inhaling nitrous oxide." I pour green tea into the blue and white Japanese teacups.

"A friend called yesterday and told me about some young men who stole a canister of nitrous oxide from a dentist's office. Police found them dead in the car the next day. Suffocated. Three kids inhaling laughing gas! What a joke—laughing gas. Maybe Jonathan's death was an accident. But then I wake up in the middle of the night wondering again—was he depressed? Why did he do such a stupid thing?" I'm crying again.

"Don't be sorry; I'm crying too." Kay leans over and hugs me.

"There's nothing you could have done," she says. "You did

everything for him, provided him with all kinds of unusual opportunities. He was a brilliant, complicated kid. You know, the minute Dave and I heard that he'd been using nitrous we started wondering. Our boys had two friends who died while inhaling nitrous. It was an accident. You mustn't go on torturing yourself."

"Yes, but when I called the police back they just said, 'Don't bother us, lady. The coroner's report is already in.' What if I'm just trying to make myself feel better? And what difference does it make anyway? Jonathan's dead, but I wish I could be sure. How can I ever know?"

"Edie, I think maybe Dave can help you. I know it won't bring Jonathan back, but Dave has influence in Sacramento; maybe he can help reopen the investigation. Maybe there's more information."

Part of me does not care. Dead is dead. No matter what we find out, Jonathan will not come back. The police did make several errors in their report. They told us they found canisters of carbon dioxide, but we learned that the cartridges were in fact nitrous oxide—laughing gas! They also made an error in the blood diagnosis. I suppose how one more kid died doesn't mean anything to them. But it does to Robin and me, and to Benji and Keshi.

That night, after the kids are asleep, Robin and I talk late into the night. He puts his arm around me. He thinks a while.

"I'll look on the Internet and get some books out from the library. Maybe Dave can help us reopen the report," he says.

I feel a tremendous relief. For the first time in months of sleepless nights, I sleep soundly.

River of Song

It is almost Easter. Keshi is gone for an overnight with her girlfriends. Robin is staying home and reading. He has a huge stack of books on the table next to the sofa. He has been reading Menninger's *Man Against Himself*, lots of books on suicide, papers from the Internet on death by nitrous oxide, books on forensic science, methods to ascertain cause of death. I am grateful he is determined to investigate. He has found more errors in the coroner's report. I cannot do this kind of research but Robin seems energized by actively trying to understand what happened. For me it is better to meditate, meet with friends, read poetry or go out and sing.

I walk toward Grace Cathedral on Nob Hill in San Francisco, with Benji. I love the crisp night air, and Benji and I hold hands, walking all the way up the long steep hill to Chinatown for dinner. We joke about how Benji acquired his taste for Chinese food from nursing. Right after his birth, a friend brought champagne and Chinese food to celebrate, and Benji has loved it ever since. After dinner we walk up the steep hill to Grace Cathedral, outlined against the darkened sky.

We do not talk much, but I can feel Benji's tender aching heart. He has gotten his growth spurt, and he is almost as tall as I am. His hair has grown down to his shoulders, and I think he is wonderfully handsome. I wonder what he thinks as we walk, but I try not to lean on him for comfort. It is easier not to talk.

Entering through the heavy Ghiberti doors, I am immediately carried into a great river of song. We join in on Bach's Cantata 140, *Sleepers Wake*. Perhaps I can find solace here. I sing for my life, tears streaming down my cheeks. Later we walk to the opposite end of the Cathedral, where a huge labyrinth awaits us: a spiral laid out upon the Cathedral floor, copied from the one in Chartres Cathedral, and used by pilgrims for centuries.

As I walk step by step through the endless turnings of the labyrinth, I begin to wonder—how might our lives be different if we had a grieving cave? I imagine myself walking down into a musky cave under the earth. There I could wail and not be ashamed of death. I could tear huge tufts of moss out by the roots. I could hurl them against the dank walls, knowing many other women would come after me.

Coming out of my reverie, I open my eyes and look up. I am stunned to see Jonathan's face again. He lingers above me under the great stone arches—luminous and smiling. Filling the entire space of the vaulted cathedral, he seems to float suspended above me, transparent. He is radiant, as if filled with light. He speaks to me again:

I'm here with you. I love you.

The sweetness in his voice goes right to my heart—a voice from long ago in his childhood, so different from his more distant young man's voice. I feel hot all over and start sweating. He stays for many minutes.

Am I losing my mind? Is this real? How could this happen again? I am not a person who sees visions. But he seems so close, so tender and alive. Jonathan, what are you trying to tell me about your life? About your death?

When finally I stumble out of the maze, I am exhausted. Benji sits cross-legged in perfectly still meditation. His eyes are shut, his head tipped slightly backward, his long blonde hair illuminated by a shaft of light. Perhaps Jonathan has come and entered right into the body of his younger brother.

I Never Knew How Much
You Loved Your Garden

Dear Jonathan,

I know it's stupid, but every time I come to Cedar Street, I turn left. Then I have to pull over to the curb. I can't drive when I've been sobbing hard. I just have to go see your house again. I have to see where you died. Remember the first time I stopped by to visit your new house and you asked if I wanted to see your garden?

"I'm in charge of watering the plants and mowing the lawn," you said, showing me every corner, every little plant and blossoming bush. Admiring three tall bushes filled with pale lilac colored blooms, you said: "This is just like the plant that grew all over at Lake Nojiri that summer we spent in Japan. What's it called in English?"

"Hydrangea," I said. "The ones in Nojiriko were all purple, and yours are purple and white. Remember the Obon Festival that summer when the entire mountainside by Lake Nojiri shook with

fireworks? The sky looked like war to me, but you were thrilled and rushed down the trail to the lake to see better."

You were so independent and self-confident in Japan. Along the little pathways, you ran from one end of the lake to the other, visiting our friends in other cabins. You'd learned that guttural talk—' Kyoto ben'—by then, and sounded just like a Japanese kid. I laughed with my Japanese women friends at your gruff imitation boy talk."

"By the way, what's the name of that bush growing on our porch at home?" you asked. "I really like the way it smells when those little white blossoms come out."

"Star jasmine," I replied.

The next time I dropped in with the excuse of bringing you a bunch of mail from our house, I brought a couple of star jasmine plants with me.

Today I parked outside your house. In front of it is a "For Sale" sign. I sneaked down the driveway, peeked into the yard to be sure no one was there, and crept through the gate, feeling like a trespasser. The star jasmine has grown, cascading over the trellis like a waterfall of tears. I had to cling to the gate so as not to faint with the familiar fragrance of those fragile white blossoms.

You never told me how much you loved your garden. Now I know.

—Your Mom

Snipping the Spider
Web Thread

Wes calls today and invites us over to visit Berkeley Systems again. He has something to show us. I call my sister El— "Can you and the kids come too? I can't bear to go there, just the four of us."

Wes greets us at the door of Berkeley Systems and takes us right to Jonathan's workstation, down the corridor past the gigantic fish tank. On the wall hang posters of the Starship Enterprise advertising the company's newest screensaver.

"Hey! Look, kids—that's the screensaver that Jonathan helped create," I say, trying not to cry in front of the cousins. I ask Wes, "Do you think we could have a copy to show the rest of the family who couldn't come?"

Jonathan's workstation looks like a hideout to me. Four makeshift walls, constructed out of moveable panels, form an inside haven for programming. He had a stereo set and professional earphones. Far Side jokes cover the walls. Hanging from the ceiling is an old computer mouse, dangling down into the middle of his office space.

"Come see the video we made," one of his colleagues says, leading us to another part of the office. "That's Jonathan's recycling project," he explains, as we look at a huge spider-web structure on the computer screen. Attached by fine threads, in a geometric design, hang cans of Pepsi, old pizza plates, and all kinds of other recyclable objects.

"Hey, isn't that Jonathan?" Lisa shouts. For a brief second on the screen, while trying to dodge the camera, Jonathan snips one thread and the entire sculpture falls to the ground. Everyone laughs.

"Edie, could you come into my office for a minute?"

Closing the door behind him, Wes reaches up and takes a large gold statue off the top of his bookshelf. It appears to be an Oscar award. But when I look closer, I see that the golden figure is holding a computer screen above his head.

Wes has tears in his eyes as he says, *Star Trek: The Screen Saver* just won the Mac User Award for the Best Desktop Publishing of the Year. You should have it. This was Jonathan's work."

The Computer Doctor

Dear Jonathan,

It's 4 A.M. again! As usual, I can't sleep, so I came to sit in the teahouse with my journal to talk to you.

Today I'm thinking about what unusual choices you made. You were determined to do things your own way! So stubborn. You never listened to a word we said. Just followed your own drummer.

During your senior year in high school, you wouldn't even look at colleges. Robin and I urged you to go through the application process at least, so your records would be on file.

"What are you planning to do after graduation?" we asked. We tried to be patient when you answered, "Oh, I'll get a job."

Get a job? With only a high school education, and no experience except working for a crazy inventor who lived in Mendocino on social security, with three goats in his yard? I remember how you met Larry at the local MAC store where computer nerds gathered on Tuesday evenings to bring problems and discoveries. You raised your hand when Larry asked for help.

You'd work late into the night on Larry's programs and try to explain to me how he was going to make a million on a new computer-typing program—back in the early days when most everyone I knew didn't even own a computer.

One day Larry showed up at the door, asking to see you. He was a foot shorter than me, had a bright red face, a prominent nose, a fluff of white hair and brilliant light blue eyes. I showed him where your room was upstairs and heard nothing for the next four hours.

"Want some supper?" I called up the stairway. No answer.

At nine-thirty that evening, Larry came downstairs. His eyes were red and he slouched, muttering, "I'm exhausted. That kid is brilliant!" After that, whenever he called he'd say: "Can I speak to your son the genius?"

Now I'm thinking—if you were so smart why the hell did you put a bag over your head!

After you died, Larry wrote us a letter. It read: "He was the brightest kid I ever met. He knew the inside of a computer like a doctor knows the human body."

He saw and appreciated in you qualities that were completely elusive and mysterious to me. Can you forgive me for living in a different world? For speaking a different language? I tried hard to understand you, dear Jonathan. Forgive me if I hurt you. I love you.
—Your wondering Mom

Mommy's Not There

Today I try to play my *koto*—Japanese zither, for the first time since Jonathan died. I can almost hear Keshi's mom Miyo encouraging me: "Don't worry, Edie, you can take a whole year to learn a piece." She was such wonderful teacher. We arranged for her to teach students in the Bay Area at our house for a week at a time, and she flew to join us from her home in San Diego every few months.

Then I remember Miyo and Robin practicing together with baby Keshi sleeping, strapped to Miyo's back. In the middle of the piece, Keshi woke up and began to cry. Robin turned off the tape recorder and they laughed.

"There's Keshi's first recording!"

It seems like another lifetime ago when Miyo and Jonathan still lived, and we all played Japanese music together. Our home reverberated with the sounds of shakuhachi, koto and shamisen, and with Miyo's haunting, deep, sonorous singing.

Miyo gave lessons ten hours a day for a week, until Saturday night when we all performed. Jonathan and Benji usually fell asleep on the floor in their pajamas. Our family life was wrapped in the warmth of Japanese music and Miyo's wise presence. Often, after the concerts, Miyo and I chatted late into the night, laughing and sharing thoughts about our children. She continued teaching and living with us every three months until she grew too weak to fly from her home in San Diego to Berkeley. Her absence left us bereft.

I shut my eyes and can almost see Miyo during those last weeks. She became blind as she lay dying. Down a long bleak darkness, she slowly, silently slipped, until not a ray of sunlight penetrated those open blinking eyes of my dear friend, my wise mentor.

The virus had entered her cornea; it burrowed right into the window of her soul.

Miyo continued playing by memory but gradually became so depleted she could no longer play at all. I flew to San Diego to be with her.

"It's dark in here," she said.

I sat in bed with her, holding her between my legs, so she could lean her back upon my breast. We talked about her death, about her hopes for Keshi. Keshi should play the violin.

"Maybe I'll be able to live until she's fourteen. Just until she's fourteen," Miyo said.

Her loving light shone out from the center of her chest. Shimmering, it cast pinwheels throughout the room, like her galaxies of music. Her soul streamed forth, as if the sheer force of her love for Keshi would vanquish the dread disease, bring back her sight, and allow her to behold her daughter grow up.

"It takes such a long time to die," Miyo sighed.

She died a week later. Ethan called us immediately, and we took the next plane down to San Diego.

When we arrived, Keshi took me by the hand right up to the bedroom where Miyo lay. She looked tiny and wizened, her cheeks sunken to the bone, her face a strange waxy yellow. Curled like a tiny fetus, she lay surrounded by Keshi's bears, stuffed penguin, several paintings and a note written in careful, fat, eight-year-old letters: I love you Mommy.

We lit candles and chanted the Heart Sutra:

Form is emptiness.
Emptiness is form.
No eyes, no nose, no ears,
No sight, no smell, no touch.

No sound, no music. No music....

"Mommy's not there," Keshi said. "She's gone. It's not Mommy."

Look! She's Shining Her Own Light

Tonight we're off to school for Keshi's spring concert. She's performing Beethoven's string quartet Opus 59, #2. How I wish Miyo could be with us.

For the first three years Keshi lived with us, she played with constricted bow strokes, her hair hanging down over one eye. Her hands felt cool and slightly limp, her head bowed with sadness.

Occasionally, on the deep low notes of the G string, or when she gained enough technique to play the slow movements of Fauré and Debussy, the most beautiful sounds poured out, filled with wordless longing.

"*Miyo, are you listening?*" I would ask silently. "*Help us. We are doing the best we can. Help her to become part of our family.*"

Soon Keshi's exceptional talent became clear. Now she is almost thirteen. She has been playing Beethoven quartets, and has performed dozens of times. Her bowing arm has strengthened and opened out, and she is beginning to stand straight and tall, instead of slumping over the violin.

Every night for the last two weeks, Keshi and Robin have been practicing in the next room while I cook dinner. I love listening to them. I can feel Robin's kind patience as he plays the piano part of the Handel violin sonata and encourages Keshi with some difficult passages and subtle interpretations. Keshi's tone is rich and deep, but suddenly they both burst out laughing when Robin messes up on a fast passage, faking a bit to keep up. For a moment, I can forget about Jonathan.

But often when Keshi performs, she seems to lose her confidence and hide her talent. Afterwards she tells us how badly she played. As we all drive to school, I can feel Keshi's nervousness. We do not talk much.

We find our seats in the auditorium and the lights dim. Robin and I hold hands as the first quartet begins. Keshi's piece is next, and Benji is backstage, warming up for the Mendelssohn Octet, the last number on the program. I can tell Robin is as nervous as I am.

Keshi leads the quartet out onto the stage, followed by the second violinist, violist, and cellist. They are all wear black skirts or black pants and white blouses and shirts. Keshi looks stunning! I know she is nervous, but it does not show. The auditorium explodes with wild applause and shouts: "Go, Keshi—Go, Marie! Joel, Jacob…"

In the darkness, my beautiful daughter seems to soar across the violin strings, her bow leaping and dancing, as her solos brazenly fill the entire hall. With her whole body, she leans into the phrases, long dark hair tumbling down over her elegant black jacket and skirt.

Miyo, listen!

I sit in darkness, tears streaming down my face. Before Jonathan's death, I do not think I ever saw Robin cry in public. I can hardly bear to look at him. I feel him shaking a little, holding in his sobs.

In the privacy of the dark auditorium, I speak silently again:

Miyo, can you hear? Look! Can you see? Our daughter is shining forth her own light.

A Stupid Mistake

Sunday morning. We sleep in and the sun warms my back. Two queen-sized pillows support me as I sit gazing out over the Bay, my grandmother's pink and purple quilt covering my feet. Robin has gone downstairs to get tea and toast. Tiger dashes in the door and jumps up onto the bed—just the way he used to when the kids were little and we all got in bed together. He purrs in the sunlight. What a relief to just sit here and do nothing. I am glad the kids are sleeping in and Robin and I have some time together. I still do not feel like making love. I just want to cry and be held.

Robin comes back, carrying a black lacquer tray, teapot, teacups and two hot scones. He talks about his research. He has been putting hours into investigating Jonathan's death, interviewing everyone who knew him. He has studied all the forensic literature on deaths associated with nitrous oxide. He has also begun to read all the books he could find on suicide, and has reviewed many medical cases of death by nitrous oxide. It seems many young people die accidentally by suffocating when they inhale nitrous in a closed environment— laughing gas and whipped cream! How absurd! Maybe his death really was an accident. A stupid mistake.

Together Robin and I have been interviewing doctors, dentists, drug experts, psychiatrists and suicidologists, as well as Jonathan's friends and coworkers. Robin plans to assemble his findings into a report Kay's husband Dave will help him present to the coroner's office.

The Light of
Hidden Flowers

Robin does not teach on Tuesdays, so we take the afternoon off to go watch Benji race cross-country with his high school team. As we drive across the San Rafael Bridge, I think about the last time I saw Jonathan running cross-country. He took a ten-day vision quest with his high school, which ended in a race over the hills of Mt. Diablo, back to the campus. He crossed the finish line minutes ahead of the second-place runner. His MAC floppy disc tied on a string around his neck flapped victoriously behind him.

Today, I say nothing to Robin as we drive through the Marin hills, which shine brightly from spring rains. It is comforting to feel so close that we need not speak, though I imagine he, too, is remembering.

We arrive at the Tennessee Valley racecourse just in time to see the kids stretching and warming up at the starting line.

Benji's team is wearing white shorts, red shirts and racing bibs with numbers. Benji is number seven. With his hair tied back in a ponytail, he is stretching out against a tree when we pull into the parking area. I am amazed at how long and lanky he has become—almost overnight! Whispers of fog float in the Pacific end of the valley. But blue sky promises warm weather for the race.

The moment I see Benji and all his friends cheering each other on, patting each other on the back, I begin to feel the delight of these healthy young athletes. I have been so impressed with the emphasis their coach puts on the importance of the kids supporting each other—downplaying competition. Their friendship and enthusiasm is contagious.

The coach blows the three-minute horn and the kids all line up, crouching down, each with one leg stretched back, heel up, ready to spring. My heart pounds with the countdown. Bang! Like a herd of colts, they stream out through the narrow valley, rounding the curve in seconds.

Robin and I hike up to the top of the hill so we can see them clearly on their return, as they loop back through the valley. The fog has lifted completely and we see the Pacific Ocean, the tips of the Golden Gate Bridge, and just a few of the tallest buildings in San Francisco. Soft new grasses cover the hills, contrasting with the deep olive green of live oaks. I pick a few purple lupines. The tiny cluster of orchid-like flowers soothes my heart.

Silence seems the most beautiful of God's music. It is a relief not to speak, and in this moment, walking together on the gentle hillside, I feel Robin's love, more tender for his sorrow. I fear I have become a plant that will never bloom again, but I know Robin sees within me the light of hidden flowers.

I thank him silently: *I am so grateful for your steady love and companionship through this gateway of grief.* For a brief moment, I feel these moist hills call forth the green sap deep within me. I want to come back to life.

"Look, Edie. Here they come. Can you see any of the numbers? Can you see Benji?"

We run down the hill to the finish line just in time to see Benji break through the ribbon, then fold over and pant as his buddies converge around him, cheering and hollering, "We won! We won! You did it, man!"

Hoisting him up, boys and girls together parade around the finish line with Benji on their shoulders.

He Was Loaned to You
for a Short Time

Soho Machida, our old friend from Kyoto, arrives for a visit. I have not seen him since our last two-year sabbatical stay in Kyoto, ten years ago. He teaches in the US now, and he looks very American with his black hair cut short, jeans and a tweed jacket over his blue shirt. He hugs me, booming forth his deep comforting laughter: "Edie, you haven't changed one bit. You're just the same!"

I am surprised he recognizes me. I think I must look like a haggard old woman.

Soho became a close friend during those two happy years of our young family life, when we felt so at home in Kyoto. He was a senior monk in the huge Daitokuji Temple complex. I used to visit the temple and quiet gardens once a week, slide aside the *shoji* door, and have tea with him while teaching him Yeats and asking questions about Zen and my Buddhist practice.

In those days, Soho often biked over to our Japanese-style

house in his monk's robes, a wool cap covering his shaven head. With his large, bald head and big ears he looked like a Buddha. He played with Jonathan, then ten years old, and with five-year-old Benji. He joined us for supper, laughed and drank lots of sake. "I thought monks didn't drink," I teased him, and poured another cup for him, Robin, and myself.

He loved hearing us practice Japanese music after supper, and when Robin played the traditional *honkyoku* monks' meditation music on his *shakuhachi* flute, Soho exclaimed: "Not even a monk could play so beautifully!"

For Robin's birthday, Soho presented us with a precious tea bowl, given to him by a famous Zen teacher. Soho was a senior monk and had the special privilege of being able to give the tea bowl a name: "I name this tea bowl in honor of you," Soho explained. "*Rei In* means Zero Sound. Because you are genius of music and mathematics." Soho bowed, filling the small *tatami* mat room with his jovial laughter.

Every week when I visited him in the temple, he showed me some of his writings. He also sent us Zen commentaries every month in his *Voice of the Frog* newsletter. His wit and brilliance impressed me: *Jiyu*; freedom. There is a Zen phrase: *Bachu jitsu getsu nagashi*—In the pot, sun and moon shine eternally. Life is a pot, which is very limited and full of restrictions. But it does not mean that we have to seek for freedom outside the pot. True freedom is nothing but our mind itself. Only if we could learn how to calm our busy mind, 'sun and moon' would start shining. Though the frog croaks a lot, what he wants to grow in his monastic pot is also freedom. That kind of freedom is, of course, available free.

Listening to Soho and reading his words always renewed my resolve to find my own freedom and peace of mind.

Now, in our living room, Soho chants the *Heart Sutra* for Jonathan. While a monk in Daitokuji Temple, he studied a special chanting technique. I have never heard such a vast, piercing sound. It begins deep down in his chest, rises in pitch as the sound engorges his throat—like a frog's dewlap—and finally pours out into the living room. I feel the reverberation in my sternum. Resonating like a great temple bell in Kyoto, Soho's voice opens a chasm of timeless spaciousness. I cry for Jonathan, yet I feel protected from the despair of grief.

When he finishes, Soho smiles and says, "Jonathan completed his life, exactly as planned. Only with our small vision do we not understand. But Buddha-eyes see. Jonathan finished his work in this lifetime. Now he is free to come back another time, without such a heavy burden. We do not know what burden he brought into this lifetime, but he came with it.

"You can analyze yourselves as parents, you can analyze his personality, but it means nothing. He came into this world with his own karma. He was loaned to you for a short time— shorter than many other children. And he completed his work.

When I chant, I get a feeling. I can tell that Jonathan is happy. It is those of you left behind who are sad. But he is fine. There is no heavy cloud in this room, in your house. Now you are mourning, but someday you will see the gift of his life."

That night, Robin and I lie like two monks in our sanctuary of kindness. I remember Naomi Nye's words:

Before you know kindness as the deepest thing inside,
you must know sorrow as the other deepest thing.

Is this Jonathan's gift?

The comfort of Robin's warmth soothes me. I curl into the familiar spoon of his embrace. Not a flicker of desire ruffles my refuge. I wonder, will I ever feel like making love again? Or did my libido die along with Jonathan? None of the grief books say much about sex.

Wings as Wide as The Sky

Dear Jonathan,

Soho came to visit yesterday. He asked if we'd kept that model airplane you made. He reminded us what good friends you were with the old man who ran the model store just around the corner from our house in Kyoto. I was always surprised that you were able to talk with him and buy all the supplies you needed. One day when I was shopping for groceries on my bike, I stopped by Kimura san's store, and there you were, perched on a stool in your baseball cap asking him to help you figure out why your model airplane motor wouldn't start.

"Let's go fly my plane today," you said, the following Saturday morning. We all piled into our tiny Honda. The wingspan of your white plane took up the whole back seat, where you scrunched in sideways, your remote control on your lap. Benji and I doubled up in front, and Robin drove through Kyoto's narrow streets to the school playground at the north end of the city. In the back seat, you slurped hot udon soup with chopsticks.

When we arrived at the school playground, we walked down to the far end of the playing field because it was empty and long enough to provide a runway for your plane. Benji, Robin and I stood shivering at the other end of the field, while you carefully placed the huge wings into the slot on top of the plane's cockpit, and bound them on with silk thread and glue. It seemed to take forever for the glue to dry.

"How's it going to get enough speed to take off?" Benji yelled down the field.

"Simple—I'll run halfway, and then launch it up into the air." Then you called to Robin. "Start the remote the minute it's out of my hands."

Robin wore his blue wool hat, long scarf, heavy jacket, boots, and gloves, which he took off in order to manipulate the controls. I waited nervously. You'd been working on that plane for at least a month.

You raced down the field and the white plane looked like a huge bird lifting slowly out of your hands into the air. It rose upward and then began a graceful turn, gliding on the wind current as it gained altitude.

Benji jumped up and down. "It's working! It's working," he said. The plane soared higher and higher. Then suddenly, it made a nose-dive and came crashing down. You ran over to it. One half of the wingspan had broken but nothing else. You picked it up and walked slowly back to where we stood. No one spoke.

"Let me see the remote," you said.

You pulled your pocketknife out of your pants pocket and began fixing something. "This is going to take more time than I thought. Let's go home," you said.

That afternoon you carried the plane down the street to Kimura san's shop and didn't come home until after supper. Benji and Robin went to bed and I waited up for you. In America, I would never have let you stay out so late, but in Japan, we never even locked our bikes or our door.

"He says it'll fly again perfectly fine," you mumbled as you walked in. Your light was still on at midnight, when I finally went to sleep. Goodnight Jonathan.

—Your Mom

Slipping Over a
Fragile Boundary

Dear Jonathan,

Robin and I are learning about what it's like to take nitrous. A few days ago my friend Catherine told me that she had once dated a dentist, and one evening they used a can of nitrous from his office. Catherine passed out. So did the dentist.

"But for some weird reason I threw up right into the mask!" Catherine told me. "I was conscious enough to rip the mask off my friend's face. That's the only reason we didn't die. God we were such fools. But the high was fabulous. I would have loved it to last forever. I can really understand what Jonathan must have felt."

Jonathan—I can actually remember the first time I had "laughing gas" at the dentist's office. I think I was about fourteen and I laughed hilariously. I loved the sensation of floating up out of myself. I remember being sad to return when the dentist finished.

The more information Robin and friends offer, the more I think you were just experimenting with a drug, discovering new altered states. Did you stride forth, out to the edge of consciousness, exploring the far reaches of the stars and your soul? Did you go too far and slip over a fragile boundary without even knowing it?

　　—*Your Mom*

Summer

Opening The Door
of My Heart

Summer is here already. Yesterday we took Benji to the airport to join the rest of the Oakland Youth Orchestra and embark on their European summer tour. We worked all spring with Benji and all the other families in the orchestra to raise money for the tour.

Keshi is going to summer camp, and Robin is happy to have a break from teaching mathematics so he can complete his report on Jonathan's death. Our living room looks as if he has borrowed a whole section of the UC Berkeley library: piles of books on suicide, forensic science, and accidental death, as well as the papers he has printed from the Internet. He plans to send his report to the coroner's office next week. It will request that they reopen our case.

"The overwhelming conclusion of these investigations," it reads, "is that Jonathan had no intention of dying; that he was using nitrous oxide as a recreational drug and was unaware of the danger as he made a fatal mistake—he attempted to prolong the high by using a garbage bag to create an extended atmosphere of gas. What he did not know was that nitrous oxide is about fifteen times more soluble in blood than oxygen, and it may quickly induce unconsciousness, so that in the absence of a sufficient oxygen supply, one can suffocate in minutes."

The report is nearly fifty pages long. It includes all the interviews with friends, colleagues, and other people we know who took nitrous as teenagers; case histories; a review of the literature; a record of Jonathan's activities in the weeks before his death (to demonstrate that his state of mind clearly indicates that his death was not intentional); and an analysis of the case, for the coroner's office. We both hope the coroner will change his report on the cause of Jonathan's death.

My friend Judith has started a summer camp on a small island in the Adriatic Sea, for child refugees of the Serbo-Croatian war. Earlier, she invited me to spend part of the summer there, teaching the children music, painting, and swimming. I accepted her invitation, and in the months since, I devoted myself to raising money to support the refugee children and the summer camp. We gave several home concerts, showed slides of the campers, and raised enough money to cover all of my expenses and send two Bosnian kids to camp. If I cannot help Jonathan, maybe I can offer something to these children.

I also receive an invitation to "take refuge" in Plum Village, the monastic community in France founded by Thich Nhat Hanh, the Vietnamese Buddhist author, peacemaker and teacher with whom I have studied extensively. The invitation is perfectly timed: I can visit Plum Village before teaching at the camp. Thinking about seeing Tây—which means Teacher in Vietnamese—gives me hope.

In the years before Jonathan's death, I contributed to our family income though my private counseling practice, and more recently with music performances and recordings. Robin and I have been thinking that it would be best for me to take a break from work for a while and live off his salary and our family savings, and I am so grateful I am able to travel. This is the first time since Jonathan left us that I have felt enough energy to do anything other than take care of everyday family life.

The last time I saw Tây and Sister Chan Khong, they were here in Berkeley when I performed on stage at the Community Theater, before his big public talk a year ago. I brought all of our rugs from the living room, and flowers from the garden, to make the stage beautiful.

I had taken the Buddhist precepts with Tây five years earlier, and had also recorded his poems with my music, so I felt blessed and privileged to perform before his Berkeley talk. I remember thinking during the performance that I had arrived at a place of inner strength: *How lucky I am to find a way to contribute to peace with music, to work with other artists in the community, for peace. Can I sustain this newfound balance and equanimity when hard times come?*

Little did I imagine that I would turn to Tây again to seek comfort and solace, but here I am, clinging by my fingernails to the remnants of a meditation practice in order to keep myself from drowning in sorrow. I am grateful for the opportunity to study with him this summer. When I feel worthless, like a failure as a mother, I remember Tây's words, and pray that I can come to accept what has happened. One of my favorite of Tây's poems keeps me afloat, like a small life raft:

> My joy is like Spring, so warm
> it makes flowers bloom all over the Earth.
> My pain is like a river of tears
> so vast it fills the four oceans.
>
> Please call me by my true names,
> so I can hear all my cries and laughter at once,
> so I can see that my joy and pain are one.
>
> Please call me by my true names,
> so I can wake up
> and the door of my heart
> could be left open,
> the door of compassion.

Can I ever open the door of my heart again?

Unbearable Pain
Becomes Its Own Cure

I have been in Plum Village in France for two days. When I first saw Tây, I could hardly say a word to him. He greeted me, bowed, and said, "Your son is here." Nothing more.

Sister Chan Khong folded her long brown robe around me with a hug. She listened patiently while I spoke of Jonathan's death, of my own confusion, pain and regrets. She offered neither advice nor interpretation. When I thanked her, she replied: "We love your music. Would you like to play in the Meditation Hall this afternoon during relaxation?"

Settling into the daily monastic schedule, I begin to feel comforted by the Sangha of monks and nuns. I sense a shift. Their practice of loving kindness begins to enter into my body. Can I learn to have compassion for myself?

How long will it take to boil the grief off my bones? Could I be like wind, blowing across these rolling vineyards? Could I become transparent as water? How long must I wait for shame and sorrow to fall away, until only kindness remains?

I have seen this wisdom in the eyes of my Vietnamese sisters—those who fled their war-torn country and now live permanently in Plum Village. They do not avert their eyes when we work in the garden together. I stoop down comfortably to weed between the rows of silky new lettuce leaves. A nun silently weeds in the row next to me, and I cry.

I am grateful to smell this good dark earth, to feel the warm summer sunlight on my back, to weed next to this Sister who fled after the Tet Offensive. I think of the garden I am building at home in Berkeley—a memorial walking meditation garden for Jonathan. I tell the nun how glad I am to work here with her in the garden. I tell her about Jonathan's death and about the garden I am building. She smiles and says: "When you are working in the garden I am happy. When I come to the garden and see this flower"—she holds a yellow chrysanthemum in her hand—"I think of you, and I am happy."

My Vietnamese sisters embrace me silently. These women, who have carried their dead brothers across the rice fields, need not speak a word of their suffering. Their deep brown eyes and steady glances assure me. *We know your grief. We embrace your suffering. We know one day your laughter will burst forth, bright as a sunflower. Be patient. Your son is here, in the vineyards, in the fields of sunflowers, in the rolling hills of summer wheat. Hear him singing in the trees, thundering through the skies with rain-storms.* Be patient, sings the sparrow. Be patient, chants the chorus of cicadas in the warm, fragrant evenings.

Breathe and Smile

This morning I walk down the dirt road through the brimming vineyards to the next village. Pungent with warm grapes, the air is thick enough to drink. Fields of bright sunflowers turn their faces in the same direction, smiling and breathing, and I hear nothing but my own slow footsteps. Breathing in, I smile; breathing out, I know I am alive. I wish I could stay here all summer. Escape all my doubts. No responsibilities. No need to explain. Just meditate, walk, breathe and smile—or at least try to.

I feel like a different person here, speaking French. I remember my freshman year of college studying abroad. Hard to imagine—I was then just a year younger than Jonathan was when he died. The world was full of adventure, music and what felt like limitless possibilities. After I started dreaming in French and began performing with the university orchestra in Lausanne, I felt completely at home. Now, the smells and warm summer sounds remind me of that carefree year.

Just as I started my year abroad, Robin and I met up in Paris and had dinner in a café by the Seine. We had grown up together in Cambridge, next door to each other. He had lived abroad as an exchange student throughout his senior year in high school, and we had been corresponding. We arranged to meet for dinner just as he finished his year abroad and I started mine. We were so innocent! How I wish he were here now. I wonder if he's heard anything from the coroner's office.

When I get back to the dining hall for lunch, one of the nuns calls me.

"*Edie, c'est ton mari qui t'appelle. Viens vite.*" Edie, your husband's on the phone. Come quickly.

I close the small door of the telephone booth and pick up the phone. "Robin—I was just thinking about that dinner we had in Paris so long ago. How did you know to call?"

Silence. I wonder if he has been disconnected.

Then in a soft voice Robin says, "Guess what? The coroner..." Robin's voice chokes to a whisper.

I cannot speak. Suddenly I hear again those words I cannot get out of my head: "*No, he's not all right. He killed himself last night.*" Leaning against the side of the now steaming hot phone booth, I'm suffocating in the silence. I want to scream: "What! What! Tell me. Hurry up! What did they say?"

Finally, Robin is able to continue, "The coroner's office changed the report. It now says 'Accidental Death.' The officer thanked me for the report and all the research. He said they'd share our findings with other coroners' offices, that maybe it would help to avoid similar errors."

Idiots, I wanted to scream into the phone. *Why the hell didn't they pay attention in the first place!*

I burst into tears and bite my tongue.

"Thank God! But how could they have done this to us? I kept wondering if they were wrong. Why didn't I listen to myself sooner? Why didn't you listen to *me* right away when I started doubting?" I hardly knew what I was saying.

"I did listen to you," Robin continued, calmly. "Why do you think I've been working so hard to find out what happened?"

"Oh, Robin, forgive me! I'm really grateful that you were so diligent, and that you insisted they reopen the investigation. It's just that I'm pissed! And relieved. And furious. And Jonathan's still dead. But it does make some difference, doesn't it? Doesn't it?"

"It won't bring him back," he says. "But it makes a big difference to me. And I think it will to Benji and Keshi."

I hang up the phone and stare at the sign with a smiling face pasted on the wall of the telephone booth with Tây's words: "Breathe and Smile."

In My Heart
Forever Lovely

I must be nuts to imagine I can help kids in the middle of a war. The overnight train clickety-clacks through the French vineyards on its way to Italy, where I will catch a boat and go on to Croatia. Even with Tây's teachings to strengthen me, will I have anything to offer the Bosnian and Croatian children from refugee camps? Can I forget about Jonathan for just a while? The moment I step off the boat onto the island of Badija, on the Adriatic, my tears begin to vanish.

By the third day on the island, war seems far away. Each day I swim, play my flute to wake the refugee children, and sing and paint with them on the patio. There are seven ten-year-old girls in my group. Some do not know how to swim, so I rock them in my arms and swish them through the balmy Adriatic waters.

Today Anna stops clutching onto me like a drowning kitten. I gently turn her on her stomach, hold her under her ribs, and guide her arms to dog paddle. She finally relaxes and even laughs: "Look! I'm swimming, I'm swimming!"

I have become close friends with Amra, Mirsada, and Amira, three young Muslim women who were able to sneak out from Sarajevo through the tunnel under the airport to join us. Mirsada cannot believe she can take a warm shower: "This is the first time in three years I have had the use of a shower. It's so wonderful!"

She tells me of dodging sniper fire to get water every morning, and how she and her friends are determined to continue studying by candlelight, huddled in small groups in the basement. My own sorrows are put in perspective as I listen to these stories and work with the children.

These silky days of summer unfold like fragrant roses. Maybe I bring comfort to some other mother, who knows her child is safe here on this island at least for a while.

During the morning, I teach the youngest children how to swim. I can imagine the healing warm waters of the clear Adriatic washing away some of their grief, as it does mine. In the afternoons, Mirsada and I set up an outdoor painting table where the children can paint their feelings and impressions of war. We help them write small poems to go with their paintings, which we display in the dining room each evening.

We have just received news that the children's paintings and poems will be featured in an exhibit in Sarajevo, the capital of Bosnia. Alongside pictures of guns, and planes dropping bombs, are poems, and paintings full of flowers, rainbows and the ocean, which show hope and their longing for peace.

Each morning before the children wake, my three new friends and I walk around the island to a protected cove, just as the crickets start singing. There, by the rocky shore, we put out a rainbow cloth and four rainbow candles. My friends teach me how to wash and prepare to offer Muslim prayers. I share teachings I have learned from Tây and tell them stories of my Quaker ancestors. We share our hopes and sorrows, then swim in the warm soothing ocean—so clear we can see the round white stones eight feet below, so buoyant we float as if dreaming on clouds. The war is far away.

The sounds of sleep breathe through the darkened monastery, our home for these two weeks. I look out my balcony window at the clear, star-filled sky, smell the fresh salty breeze, and walk down the corridor to Mirsada's room. We are just finishing the translation of thirteen-year-old Jelika's poem, so we can put it up on the dining room wall in the morning. She writes:

> *Maybe some people destroyed this world*
> *But in my heart it is forever lovely*
> *As a spring flower.*
> *Maybe they burned all,*
> *But our memories do not burn.*
> *They are radiant and eternal.*

Memories stay hidden in our hearts

Like the biggest secret.

Maybe they destroyed our reality.

They can change our future but not our past.

Because the past is our treasure

And we keep the past and our memories

Because they are beyond any price.

Maybe The Worst Is Over

As I settle into life at home, I feel surprisingly refreshed and rested by my trip. Robin and Keshi have flowers in the living room to welcome Benji and me, and this morning we're celebrating being together with a leisurely Sunday brunch.

The sun streams into the kitchen, and our front garden blooms with dahlias, orange nasturtiums creeping over the stones, and Jonathan's yellow rose bush. We open the French doors and set the table with a yellow and orange flowered tablecloth. No rush today, so we can enjoy being together. We imagine we're in a café with French omelets, fresh scones, home-squeezed orange juice and English breakfast tea. This is our Berkeley café, chez Hartshorne.

Robin has begun work on a new book on Euclid, and we sense his excitement. A brown package arrived in the mail yesterday from England. After breakfast, we all go into the living room, so the package will not get food on it, and Robin carefully cuts the brown paper while we watch. Under layers of wrapping paper and old newspapers nestles a fat book in its original tan vellum binding. As Robin carefully opens to the frontispiece, I see traces of hungry worms having munched deep trails in the pages.

"It must be a delicious book," I kid Robin. "What's it about?"

He opens the book, carefully inspects the elaborate frontispiece, and reads aloud: "Euclidis Elementorum, Libri XV, 1574."

He grins, and pats the book affectionately. "I got it from my antique book dealer in England."

Though I cannot understand a word of the books and research papers Robin writes on algebraic geometry, I love looking at the drawings in this beautiful ancient text.

He opens to page seventy-two. "See, here's the Pythagorean theorem, Book I, Proposition 47."

I marvel at the symmetry and detail of the hand-drawn geometric triangle with squares on each side. Though I never liked math in school, I can feel the beauty and simplicity of this book, and Robin's excitement is infectious. I'm happy to see him return to his passion for mathematics.

Keshi teases Robin about his latest collecting hobby. "Robin, don't you think a new dress and matching necklace for me would be a bargain compared to that little book?"

I catch myself wondering if it is okay to laugh. *Jonathan, I wish you were here too.*

It is good to be home. I hope that coming back renewed from travels will make life a little easier here in Berkeley. Maybe the worst is over.

Nothing Is the Same

My heart aches as we drop Benji off at the San Francisco airport. He has gone off to Vermont for a semester at the Mountain School. Our home will seem empty without him, our family smaller. But I am glad he will have a respite from the grief that Robin and I still have trouble hiding.

After saying goodbye, I close my eyes and imagine him driving up to the Mountain School, past the old red barn with cows and chickens, past the duck pond and fruit trees. Like a delicious summer fruit, Benji is tan and golden and seems filled with sunshine when he waves to us.

Fall always used to feel like a fresh start, but now nothing is the same. The excitement of beginning anew, while basking in the fullness of harvest and crisp evenings, is gone. My old patterns do not work anymore. It is a struggle to know who I am.

While Keshi goes out shopping for school clothes, and Robin prepares for classes, I walk down to Solano Avenue to get a cup of chai at Peet's. It's a wonderful Indian summer morning, warm enough still to wear my yellow sunflower dress. At Peet's, I bump into my poet activist friend Judith.

"Edie, I'm so glad you're back!" She hugs me warmly. "Guess what? I have the most exciting news! Andrea's engaged and she'll be getting married next spring. We just went out shopping for her wedding dress, and she looks adorable! Can you imagine—my baby is all grown up?"

"Oh, that's just fabulous!" I turn to pour milk in my tea so Judith won't see the tears in my eyes.

I am embarrassed. I love Judith and she has been such a loyal friend this year I am happy for her—we've known Andrea since she was born. She and Jonathan attended a playgroup together. Jonathan will never marry.

Walking home I wonder, *how long will it be before I can enjoy other people's happiness?* Will I ever again celebrate the precious events of our human lifetimes without pain piercing my heart?

Peonies Bouncing Their Splendor

To my relief, Keshi seems to be enjoying high school. Jonathan has been dead for nine months. Mostly I am able to keep my sadness to myself, but I still worry that I am not always available for her. Nighttime is the hardest. At least during most of the day I seem to be functioning again. I love being with the kids. While Benji is away at the Mountain School, I enjoy Keshi's great group of friends. This week I helped her prepare for her fourteenth birthday party, and because Robin is in Paris giving a talk, we have an all-female household.

To celebrate this rite of passage, Keshi has invited fourteen young women friends—artists, poets, painters, actresses all—to a performance party:

If you are a poet, bring a poem,
If you're a musician, bring a song,
If you're an actress, bring an improvisation,
But most of all, bring yourself

To celebrate my 14th birthday.
For women only! (Thank Goodness)

Keshi and I have spent the last two days preparing the house. Crystal glasses sparkle on the lace tabletop in the late afternoon sunset; tall taper candles await the guests' arrival.

Keshi returns from her shopping expedition looking a little nervous. "The good news is it'll only cost twenty dollars, not sixty, to replace that video the VCR ate up. The bad news is that the flowers cost sixty-four dollars."

"What?"

"Well... " She looks abashed. "I didn't ask how much they were ahead of time, and after the flower lady cut them, I didn't think I could say anything." Keshi peeks through the flowers: full-breasted peonies, bouncing their splendor and swirling their fragrance wantonly; young white lilies, skin transparent as a girl's; fragile purple orchids, hovering like hummingbirds. A bursting armful of joyous abundance, announcing Keshi's delight. The flowers cover the entire top half of her body, and encircle her beautiful moon face. She has pulled her long black hair into an elegant bun at the nape of her neck.

Well, she's only fourteen once, I think, backing down a bit. All afternoon we have been cooking with Keshi's two best friends. Janna is making a chocolate cake: eighteen inches in diameter, in three dense layers filled with heavy, thick chocolate cream and decorated with strawberries and nasturtiums from the garden.

At four o'clock, the doorbell rings. Everyone arrives at once. The feast is ready: half a salmon poached in white wine and fresh tarragon, basted with spicy Dijon mustard; strawberry soup, two kinds of salad, and penne pasta for the vegetarians. The girls toast Keshi with sparkling amber grape juice in crystal glasses. They are brimming with poems and stories and jokes.

"I have the most wonderful friends in the world!" Keshi raises her glass to each one.

When Keshi first came to us she suffered from shyness and had only one or two friends. This year, she wrote her first poem, "Chap Book," about her parents' dying. One of her teachers invited her to speak in front of the freshman health class about death. Last week, for the first time, she made the honor roll, and now here she is, glowing with the recognition and love that fourteen young women friends bestow upon her.

I am witnessing a girl crossing the threshold to young womanhood. It seems like a wedding celebration, and I sense Miyo's presence, here beside me. *Miyo, behold our beautiful young daughter! She is transforming sorrow into beauty and wisdom. Can I ever do the same?*

As the sun sets behind the Golden Gate Bridge, the young women light the candles, and each offers her gift. Keshi has set my place between two of her best friends. Janna dances a slow solo on her toe shoes, her young body a cornucopia of beauty, arching backwards with prefect precision. Eileen plays the Irish harp and sings, her brilliant straight red hair shining in the candlelight. Esther sings a song she has composed in French, of love and longing, and sounds exactly like Edith Piaf. Elyia recites a monologue from *Love's Labor's Lost*, and Rosie reads original poems from her journal. Keshi plays the slow movement from the Bach D Minor unaccompanied violin sonata. Our living room resonates with the hush of her admiring friends and her deeply colored phrases. *Miyo, are you listening?*

While clearing the dishes and washing up, I overhear snippets of laughter and stories, then a long conversation about death. Keshi doesn't say much, and I wonder how she feels hearing this discussion.

Suddenly, Janna and Marie run upstairs, and I run after them. I can hear Keshi sobbing through her closed bedroom door. I knock and hear a muffled "Come in." Janna and Marie are sitting on the bed, on either side of Keshi. I get right into bed with her and hug her against my body.

"I am so sorry, dear, dear Keshi, that you have to suffer this pain. I know it doesn't go away."

"You are so incredible, the way you handle everything," Marie says to Keshi. "Sometimes we forget." They hug her.

"I don't mind your talking about my parents dying," Keshi says. It was the part about the drugs. If there'd been drugs earlier, they could have lived. They could have been here to see me turn fourteen."

After a short while, Keshi and her friends rejoin the party, and as I go off to bed, drifting into sleep, I hear them chatting and laughing far into the night. I lie in wonder and gratitude at the gift of this remarkable young woman. Keshi has a lot to teach me. Perhaps I am not such a failure as a mom after all.

On the Curbstone

For a short period after Keshi's party, I enjoyed our family life again, but now I can barely carry on. When will the grief end? When I try to lead a normal life, I fall flat on my face. Every day I meditate and write in a journal before I see clients, go to rehearsals, try to keep up with the mail, bills, and family needs. But some days I am immobilized.

My body can hardly rise out of weary torment. Is it enough that I simply get out of bed and remain upright? Get dressed, make sandwiches for school? Sit quietly, meditating in the teahouse with Judith, Catherine and Kay – members of our sangha—who come by every morning at 7:30 A.M.?

Today I can barely contain my sobs until they leave the teahouse and drive away. My son is dead. My son is dead. My dream is dead. My grandchildren are dead. My longing is dead.

Is it self-indulgent to feel that I must stay deeply connected to my longing, grief, and sorrow for Jonathan? This seems to be my only authentic self at this moment, no matter what the "stages of grief" are supposed to be. In a few months, Jonathan will have been gone for a whole year. Books on grief say I should be re-engaging with life by now—whatever that means. Isn't it bad enough that he's dead? Do I have to heap ashes over my head and make it worse? Oh God, I wish I had some wisdom.

On the outside, I appear to manage. But inside, much of the time I still feel shattered, crazed, unable to sustain a single thought for even a moment. When no one is around, I wander through rooms in the house and cannot remember what I came for. I start sentences and cannot end them. I forget the names of close friends, the names of streets.

I wake up in the morning drenched with fear that my life as I knew it is seeping away. Not only have I lost my son, but I am also losing the purpose and substance of my own life. For the first time, I am very afraid; afraid that what little security I have left will also vanish, that Robin will die. Benji will eat a poison mushroom while on his vision quest at the Mountain School. Keshi will be hit by a car. The house will burn down. I will be reduced to a gray-haired, ranting old woman on the curbstone.

Soul Dream

I dream that Jonathan makes elaborate preparations for using nitrous oxide. He is much like himself: totally focused, taking great care, and tending to the details. The apparatus is complex and intricate. He is precise, in control, and he enjoys himself. Suddenly his soul leaves his body, and at that moment, he hears voices calling him to come onward. Others call him back: "Don't leave. Don't leave yet. It's too soon."

He makes a definite choice and follows the voices from beyond. I sense no sadness or despair in this choice. He is very attracted and curious. He leaves and goes toward the light. There is only bright yellow light.

I wake up. In my half-dreaming state, I feel calm and warm throughout my body, almost as if I'm being rocked in the summertime of my childhood. I float on my back, drift along with the current, look up at the clouds. Jonathan, perhaps you are guiding me.

When No One Speaks

"We're here!" My younger brother, Fred, booms this out as he slams the rickety screen door on our family home on Cape Cod. "Andy and Chris and Ginny and Kate were all following us, and Hal and Nannie and the other kids started a little after them. They should be here any minute." He gives me a big hug. "How was thy trip? Good to see thee. I'm so glad you could all come East for Thanksgiving. Hey—it's the big Benji! Where's Keshi?" Fred continues gathering the family together—just like my father, I think, remembering funny moments when Dad danced with my cousin on the dining room table; when he taught the entire fire department how to trampoline out in the backyard.

Outside, honking and slamming car doors announce the arrival of everyone else. Ali and Chris lug in bags of food, and Hal pushes the wheelchair while my mom insists on walking in on her crutches, which clatter to the floor the minute she sits down in the kitchen. "Whew. I'm pooped," she puffs. "Oh my goodness, it's Edie and Robin too! Where in the world did you come from?" Mom's memory is gone. She has totally forgotten that we were flying east for Thanksgiving.

We unload the cars and all pile into the kitchen. "I brought a keg of beer," Eric laughs. He sets up the jug and hands everyone a drink. Everyone talks at once, as we chop vegetables, make the salad and dust off the dishes. "How many should I set for?" Andy asks. He's brought his golden lab puppy, and the dogs all race from the kitchen into the living room and back.

"Hey Benji, how about a run to work up that appetite?" Ali calls. Keshi and Anita stay to help in the kitchen, while four of the cousins and Benji follow Ali, each one slamming the door. "See you in an hour; we won't be eating before then, will we?"

I go into the parlor and watch them stream down the street, the salty water and marsh grass beyond them barely distinguishable from the sleet-gray sky. They all have such a familiar look—long lean muscles and the athletic build of my dad. Square jaws, even on the girls, and rows of bright white teeth, blond or light brown hair. What a clan they are. And I am happy for Benji, despite the ache I feel when I see them disappear around the bend without Jonathan.

Shining with the confidence of young love and a bright future, the kids return just in time to sit down at the long table, now filled with turkey, creamed onions, sweet potatoes, beans, cranberry dressing, salad, and wine. We all hold hands Quaker style for a moment of silence. Then a cacophony of hungry enthusiasm: "Chow down! Pass the turkey. Smells great! Get your dog out from under my legs, will you? It's not my dog, it's yours. Mine is well trained!" The conversation grows louder and no one listens. I ring a glass, make a toast, and ask each cousin: "What's special in your life right now?"

Eric is the first to reply, raising his wine glass to make a toast: "Nanny, thee's going to be a great-grandmother; is thee ready?"

"I'm going to be a *what*?" Her croaky voice calls across the immense mahogany dining table.

"Turn on thy hearing aid, Nanny." Eric grins, now bright red. "Thee's going to be a great-grandmother!"

No one says a word about Jonathan's absence at dinner, not even during the blessing. I am crushed. How can they forget so easily? Why is it so hard to speak aloud of death, of grief?

Later in the evening, I talk with my mother, tell her of my disappointment.

"*Of course* we were all thinking of Jonathan! How could thee imagine otherwise? Maybe they thought it would just upset thee if anyone spoke of him."

I know she is right. I wonder how to tell my family and others that it is much more painful when no one speaks.

Jonathan's Garden Is Blooming!

I'm back in Berkeley. My friend Kay just called and asked if she could drop by. I have not seen her since she and Dave helped us reopen the coroner's report. I have been fighting off depression again. All week I have been dreading tomorrow—the first anniversary of Jonathan's death. I keep hearing those awful words on the phone again, and yet it might have happened a lifetime ago. And an instant ago. Everyone else's life goes on as usual. Not mine.

We settle into the sagging, comfortable sofa. Kay says, "Jonathan's spirit came and visited me in a dream. He couldn't get through to you because your grief is too intense, so he came to me. I looked out the large plate glass window in your house at Jonathan's garden. The garden bloomed brilliantly, with every kind of flower and every imaginable color –daisies and daffodils, crocuses and magnolias and azaleas. All in bloom.

"I said to you: 'Edie, look! Jonathan's garden is blooming.

And look! There are even dahlia buds about to come forth. Dahlias never bloom at this time of year.' He's sending you a message—he's flowering, he's wonderfully happy and full of color."

"Do you really think he's blooming, Kay?" I'm relieved that I don't have to apologize for crying so openly. "I pray you're right. Tomorrow a group of my Berkeley women friends are coming to plant bulbs in Jonathan's garden."

After Kay leaves, I wonder, would Jonathan come to me again, if only I could stop crying?

Kimono with a Silver Obi

We decide to spend Christmas in Japan with Keshi's family. Keshi's obasan was unable to visit Miyo in America, even as Miyo lay dying. Obasan sent her daughter healing herbs and wrote to her: "You are not going to die. A daughter may not die before her mother."

Now Miyo's mother is seventy-eight and I am fifty-eight, and we share a parent's worst nightmare.

When Keshi was little, Miyo said to me, "Keshi is just like my obasan—her great grandmother. Stubborn and strong-willed!" In the bathtub when she was not yet two, Keshi refused to sit down to be washed. She folded her arms and said defiantly: "Stand up for bath!"

Obasan waits to greet us at the gate of her home in Okazakura. She is short and quite plump, dressed in a dark gray kimono with a silver obi. Subtle patterns of waves and chrysanthemums weave through the heavy silk of the obi, which probably belonged to her mother, Keshi's great-grandmother, the stubborn, well-known teacher of tea ceremony. I see that Obasan looks away and has tears in her eyes. We hug and I know now how she has suffered.

Keshi's four cousins, aunt, and uncle crowd around, greeting her in English and Japanese and exclaiming how grown up she has become since her last visit, at age six. Both Benji and Keshi have studied a little Japanese in school, and Robin speaks fluently, while I bumble along with polite "women's talk."

Almost immediately my feet start sliding along, toes pointed inward, in small gliding steps; folding my hands politely, right over left, and bowing. I am careful to bow a bit more deeply than each member of the family. Robin and Tadaji, Keshi's uncle, stride ahead, chatting comfortably in Japanese. I feel my body drawing inward, becoming more compact—in some ways a relief, and protection, from the roller coaster of emotions during the last year. I relax in their care, marveling at the unique way Japanese friends know to anticipate every need, every desire, before it even arises.

Where Can Their
Spirits Rest?

Robin and I have been wondering when to speak of Miyo's memorial plaque. Today as we visit Keshi's grandparents' home, Obasan shows us the family *butsudan*—the gold and lacquer altar that houses memorial plaques for all deceased family members going back ten generations. Miyo's plaque is noticeably missing.

I say nothing as I gaze behind the elaborate open doors of the family *butsudan*, and I wonder if Obasan talks to Miyo.

In our home in Berkeley, we also have a *butsudan*, which I bought at a temple sale in Kyoto twenty years ago. Since Jonathan's death, several times a week I light candles and incense in front it, and I ring the small bell to let his spirit know I am calling him. Alone, I often close my eyes, pray, and talk directly to him. I also talk to Miyo's spirit and ask her for guidance in raising Keshi.

While we prepared for our visit to Keshi's Japanese family,

Robin and I had wondered if we should have a plaque for Ethan and Miyo in our *butsudan*. We had scattered their ashes with Keshi near their home after they both died, but we had no place in our home for their spirits to rest or visit us. Well aware of the bitterness Keshi's uncle felt after visiting Ethan and Miyo in America, we wondered how to approach the subject with Miyo's family. Did they want Miyo's ashes returned to them? Would they like to have a memorial plaque in their *butsudan*?

At supper, I casually invite the family to come and visit us in Berkeley and see San Francisco. Tadaji replies in a low voice, "I will never set foot on American soil again."

Bitterness and Sorrow Begin to Dissolve

Robin and I sleep until noon, awakening to find Benji and Keshi already up, watching TV in their *yukatas* with the cousins. I sink into the warm steaming *o furo*, or Japanese bath, which Haruko has prepared. For the first time in long while, I relax. Whatever anxieties Robin and I had about the family's bitterness, surrounding Miyo's death, they melt into the steaming bath. I feel at home here in Okazakura, as I did in Kyoto many years ago.

Each day the family has planned a trip to nearby temples, scenic spots, and local Okazakura specialty shops and restaurants. Tadaji is the builder for Sushihan, the most elegant Sushi shop in the city, so he invites us there for dinner. After several courses of *maguro*, *ebi*, and *tamago sushi*, our host, the owner of the restaurant, brings out *ikizukuri*, living fish that still twitches. Several cups of hot sake have dimmed my hesitation, so I politely eat this delicacy.

Tadajisan tells us a sad tale of how the last chef here died when he mistakenly ate *fugu*, blowfish,— one of the greatest delicacies of Japan. Its small poisonous pouch is located just between its gills and jawbone. Extracting the poisonous sack without rupturing it requires two years' training in a special *fugu* school for chefs. The sushi master had not quite finished his training.

After the feast, Tadaji brings out his most prized, aged Jack Daniel's and asks Robin if he would play *shakuhachi* while we all relax. Robin begins with a series of folk songs. When I had a job in Kyoto playing in the foyer of an upscale restaurant, I often played these same songs.

"*ARA—gaijin san!*" the astonished guests would say, when they walked in and saw me dressed in kimono, seated on a two-*tatami* mat dais playing the *koto*. Once when I chose to sing a particularly sad drinking song about the moon in autumn, an elderly woman, also dressed in a kimono, came and sang along with me into the mike.

Keshi's family seems equally astonished at Robin's playing. When he finishes, Tadaji exclaims, "You are more Japanese than the Japanese!"

We sense a new receptivity in the family. Perhaps this is the moment to bring up the memorial plaque for Miyo.

Robin circles delicately around the subject in very polite Japanese. He says that we also have a *butsudan* in our home, and that we wonder if Miyo's plaque should rest there with us.

No one speaks. Oh dear, I think. We blew it. How will we ever integrate our two families?

Now We Are One Family

We sleep late and I awaken to see a delicate dusting of new snow on the pine tree and camellia bushes outside our window. Robin remains asleep, but I sit up with the cozy quilt tucked around me and look out into the garden.

Our single living, dining, and sleeping room in Kyoto looked out into a similar tiny garden. For the first time in a few days, I think of Kyoto and of Jonathan. Lingering in the warmth of Robin's sleep and the fluffy down futon, I stop to remember: twenty-one years ago, I gave birth to Jonathan in Japan, and here we are again, enfolded into the lives and hearts of our new Japanese family. But with our visit over, it is time to pack our bags, now stuffed with gifts.

At the railroad station, the entire family waits with us for the long, sleek *shinkansen* to nose its way silently into the station. We bow formally to each other. I want to hug Obasan and Miyo's sister, who almost feels like my own sister now. But I restrain myself, and bow lower than they do, several times. Just before we step into the train, I bow to Tadaji and notice that he, too, has tears in his eyes.

Quietly he says, "Now we are one family."

A Resting Place

Three weeks later, in Berkeley, we receive a package in the mail, return address Okazakura. Inside the shipping box, the small item is beautifully wrapped in Ginko leaves. I am so excited I don't wait for Robin to come home from work or Keshi from school. I delicately peel back the wrapping to expose a letter, written on handmade rice paper. *Thank you for your invitation. Keshi's cousins would like to visit for a week during their spring vacation. Miyo loved America and always wanted to be buried there. We think her spirit should rest with you, in your home.*

And there, carefully cushioned in a soft yellow silk wrapping, lies a beautiful black lacquer ware plaque with gold letters. Miyo's name is on the left in Japanese characters and Ethan's name is on the right, spelled out in *katakana*, the Japanese letters for foreign words.

I walk five steps up to the front hall landing and open the

carved wooden doors of our own family *butsudan*. Next to the photo of Jonathan, I place Miyo and Ethan's plaque. I ring the small bell and light three sticks of incense. Silence and the sweet fragrance of sandalwood encircle me, filled with memories and a blessing.

Harvest

Kindness

Before you know what kindness really is
you must lose things,
feel the future dissolve in a moment
like salt in a weakened broth.
What you held in your hand,
what you counted and carefully saved,
all this must go so you know
how desolate the landscape can be
between the regions of kindness...

Before you know kindness as the deepest thing inside,
you must know sorrow as the other deepest thing.
You must wake up with sorrow.
You must speak to it till your voice
catches the thread of all sorrows
and you see the size of the cloth.

Then it is only kindness that makes any sense anymore,
only kindness that ties your shoes
and sends you out into the day to mail letters and
purchase bread,
only kindness that raises its head
from the crowd of the world to say
It is I you have been looking for,
and then goes with you everywhere
like a shadow or a friend.

—Naomi Shihab Nye

I Dream of Kyoto, Jonathan's Birthplace

I awaken from a vivid dream and can almost feel Jonathan's presence.

Dear Jonathan,

You are very close. Are you trying to speak to me? I feel the power of your birth in Japan, our time together there. What are you trying to teach me?

Orange persimmons keep a solitary vigil, hanging against black tile roofs beside the darkened temples of Kyoto. Winter rains have washed clean the leaves, now barely skeletons along the narrow passageway. The gray stone lanterns gleam their musky candlelight. It's almost night now, and chilly. The bell of Daitoku-ji Temple rumbles through my bones, muted by the soft shroud of sorrow.

Wandering through temple pathways, I listen to the pigeons call under the eaves. Jonathan, will I ever meet you again, orange persimmons lighting our way?

Today I unwrap each small fruit of your life—carefully har-
vested now, tucked away for winter in the root cellar of memory.
I sense your soul brushing my skin, dusting wings over the hair on
my arm. I begin to realize that we are here to shed the garment of
our lives, to shed our leaves. The rain is washing my heart clean
again.

Jonathan, please help me to accept what is true. I love you.

—Your Mom

Blended Families

In the shower this morning, I suddenly realize: We are a "blended family," both living and dead, combining two cultures. There are four parents, two brothers, and a sister in our family. It's just that Ethan and Miyo and Jonathan are on the other side, and we are here.

What a novel kind of family! How can we integrate our American family with Keshi's Japanese one? Who is our family now? No matter where I go, I am aware of Jonathan—of his spirit, of his life, and of the fact that he is no longer with us. I can only imagine how painful and complicated Keshi's feelings about family must be.

I pray for guidance—to have strength, compassion, and wisdom to provide a loving container for her, and for all of us. And I wonder, could my own doubts and questions support others who seek to "repair the world" after suffering a loss, perhaps one child at a time, one parent at a time, one family at a time?

Oversized Luggage
and Rose Petals

A few months later, I return from my first performance after Jonathan's death. While waiting for my *koto* to arrive at the baggage claim in the San Francisco airport, I give Mom a ring to wish her Happy Mother's Day. No answer. I wonder where she might be, maybe at my brother's? I wonder if she's thinking of me, 3,000 miles away.

I'd taken care to mark my instrument 'Fragile' and have it hand carried onto the plane. It seems to take forever, and there are almost no bags on the belt. Just then I see a service man pick up my *koto* off the belt, and dump it onto the ground, despite the red stickers screaming out for gentle handling.

He probably thinks it's a surfboard I mutter. Then I shout: "That's a precious musical instrument you just tossed!" I unzip the case, poke through the padding to see if it's cracked. I'm still fuming when Benji comes loping through the glass doors, dressed in his performance tux. He must have come straight from the Oakland Youth Orchestra performance, which I missed while I was in Santa Barbara at a peace conference. Oh why did I miss Benji's concert? Why didn't I just stay home with my kids? What kind of mom am I, anyway…

Benji gives me a big hug, grins and hands me a box of Sees Chocolates and says "Happy Mother's Day!" He hoists my flute case over his shoulder, puts the *koto* under his arm, and picks up my bag with his free hand. "The car's in the parking lot. Let's go."

At home, Keshi greets me at the door and hands me a bouquet of flowers. "Don't look in the living room. Come on up stairs," she says.

She leads me to the bathroom where a fragrant, frothy bubble bath is steaming. Fatigue and months of trying to push myself out into the world again, to piece together my shattered self esteem—all dissolve in the welcoming warmth of the bath my kids prepared for me. How do I deserve such wonderful kids? I remember Rumi's advice: *Practice gratitude and love will shine through you its all healing joy.*

Then a darkening thought arrives: "Jonathan, am I being disloyal to you, to be so happy with Benji and Keshi? Do you think I'm forgetting?' I sink deeper into the water's warm embrace. "Forgive me, dear Jonathan. I love you still. And I have to come back to life."

"Dinner's ready," Keshi calls up the stairs. Two of my three children are here! Enjoy them while you can, I remind myself.

In the living room the low Japanese table is set in front of a crackling fire, with candles and a blue vase filled with fresh narcissus. The chicken stew smells delicious. At the end of the table, spelled out in rose petals is my welcome: HAPPY MOTHER'S DAY.

A More Authentic Image

Time passes more quickly now. Pink clouds of plum blossoms float through the rains in. Berkeley, where spring blooms in early February. I feel young new seeds thrusting their roots into the rain-soaked soil of winter, as if the lengthening sunlight calls me back to life after this long period of gestation, of dwelling in darkness. Where will it lead me? I feel my roots strengthened, stirring with new life. As spring gardens rejoice all over the Berkeley hills, I return to Cambridge in Boston to celebrate my mother's birthday.

As we fly over the snow-covered Sierras, I remember Thich Nhat Hanh's teaching that we have three root sources: our biological family, our heritage of culture and religion at birth and our chosen spiritual path. We need to embrace all three. As a young woman, I left my origins, those roots of my land and my genetic inheritance. I longed for the artistic, sexual, and spiritual awakenings that seemed like forbidden fruit in the garden of my Cambridge Quaker upbringing.

Gazing out at the sparkle of the Sierras far below, I imagine speaking to my Mom:

Well, Ma, what would thee think of rose petals, like a secret code enciphering my longing for mother-love, for daughter-love. And what if I bought thee an extravagant bouquet of red roses, then one by one plucked off each petal, placed it on thy dining room table, declaring: "I love thee!"

What would thee think of my longings for freedom and artistic expression? What would thee say of my determination to look death right in the face? Each time I come for a visit I wonder If I can finally reveal my true self. Will thee ever see me?

The pilot announces our descent into Boston and I peer out into the blackness, hoping to see the shoreline and the familiar harbor welcoming me back to my East Coast roots. Heavy clouds, then snow obscure my view.

It's still snowing when I get into the Boston cab. Along Storrow Drive, the lights of MIT and the Harvard towers twinkle like stars in the Charles River. Puffs of cold air sting the inside of my nose, bright and familiar, waking me up. I'm coming home again. Sleeting city snow reminds me also of winters so long ago in Japan, snow falling outside the *shoji* of the tiny Japanese house, where we brought newborn Jonathan home from the hospital. Strange how coming home always evokes these old memories.

Since Jonathan's death I've become more aware that Kyoto and our life in Japan offered a gateway to my spiritual path. Immersion in that culture also reminds me of much that I cherish from my Quaker New England heritage: a love of nature and feeling rooted in the cycle of changing seasons, attention to detail, discernment, and moral commitment to the well-being of others. How I long to integrate the many roots of my journey so I can bloom again. On this visit, Mom will attend my talk at the Peace and Social Justice Committee Meeting at the same Quaker Meeting House I attended as a child. I am pleased she will be there to witness me talking about the work to which I have devoted myself for the last fifteen years. Despite our closeness, she has never truly acknowledged this part of me. Out of the darkness of death, I sense new patterns emerging, a new mirror for my soul. I am piecing together again the shattered fragments of my life. Could a mirror that has been broken and mended reflect a more authentic image?

Gathering Lost Fragments

The taxi takes me to 35 Lake View Avenue, the old brick house in Cambridge, where I grew up. It is after midnight, dark and the brick sidewalk is icy. I turn the key quietly, wondering if Mom is asleep. I sneak into the living room, turn on the lights and look at all the photos of us as kids, photos of weddings, Mom holding grandbabies, and Jonathan. The house smells of my childhood.

My brother Hal, the doctor, said Mom was well enough to come home from her last operation. I peek into the room where I can hear her snoring. She looks small and helpless curled up on her side, her mouth open. I resist waking her, knowing that she will be disoriented and that she needs her sleep.

I have said goodbye to her many times now. Each time she is hospitalized, I wonder if she will recover. Her support has meant so much: I cannot bear to let her go, so close to Jonathan's leaving. Yet still there is much unspoken between us.

I wake early to see snow slanting through a shaft of street light just outside my window. I jump out of bed, and put on the long red underwear Mom has laid out for me. She sleeps soundly, so I go for a walk before breakfast.

In this silent early morning, light snow falls like tiny slivers of silver mirrors all about me. It is eight degrees. The air stings my breath on the intake. Ice and snow crunch beneath my fur-lined boots as I walk down Brattle Street toward Harvard Square. These footsteps seem imprinted in the bones of my feet. I feel as excited as the first time I walked down this same street alone—big enough to go to school all by myself, wearing my new snow jacket with the red fuzzy hood.

Continuing down Brattle Street, past Longfellow House, I turn into the park of the Quaker Meeting House. It snowed when Robin and I married here twenty-seven years ago. Stepping inside, I remember the crackling fire, the embracing silence of the Quaker meeting and the circle of friends and family. I can almost see my grandmother Bema shining, her white hair gathered in a tight bun at the nape of her neck. Her wise words guide me still: "Follow thy inner light, dear. It is thy greatest treasure."

I feel the old comfort of belonging here with my ancestors, and I gather in some lost fragments of myself.

I leave the quiet of the meetinghouse and walk past the skating club where Mom taught me how to waltz to Tchaikovsky, winging our way across the sleek, silvery ice. I remember how free of doubt and regrets I felt then. Gazing out at the empty dark rink, I see myself with my mom, and I remember the first time she allowed me to skate at night for the waltz competition.

With her little plaid hat and short gray skirt, my Mom twirls me and holds me as I glide backwards, then around in a figure three to the long arc onto one foot, slicing the ice with the outer edge of my skate, my other leg like an arrow shot straight out behind me. I am proud and confident to be so grown up that I can dance at waltz night.

My mom's sturdy Yankee courage, I think to myself. I wish she would pass some of it on to me! Somehow, I feel my bones grow stronger as I skid on the icy brick sidewalk down Brattle Street, returning home.

I get back just in time to hear Mom talking to herself upstairs. I go to help her get dressed, and she looks surprised, and then happy to see me. I turn my eyes away from her ribs sticking out, from her single sagging breast and from the long scar where the right breast once rested.

As I help her on with her bra, she corrects me in a way that makes me feel little again. "Thee's got my boob on the wrong side! Here. I'll do it." She takes the false foam breast out of the left bra cup and slips it into the right. "I'd be double breasted the way thee was going! Hand me my crutches, will thee?"

She walks unsteadily toward the stairs.

I suggest she use the recently installed chair to ride down.

"I can perfectly well walk downstairs, thank thee," she says, without smiling, and slowly, step-by-step, she clomps down the stairs.

Red Cow Emerges from The Forest

When I visit Cambridge, I always look forward to taking the studio art class with my mom. If she could start painting when she was eighty-one, I reason, surely I can start in my fifties. It is snowing again when we get up, but Mom is determined to go to the class. I shovel off the sidewalk and the wooden ramp my brother built so Mom could roll her wheel chair up and down the two steps to her house. As we eat breakfast, Mom drops her hearing aid onto the floor.

"Damn! It's such a nuisance to have all these removable parts!"

"Here it is Mom; it rolled under thy chair. Want some help getting it in?"

"No thank thee. I can do it myself. But where are my glasses? I *know* I left them in my purse. Did thee move them?"

"No, Mom. Thee left them in the bathroom." I go to look for them. When I come back, Mom rolls her way toward the front door, struggling to put on her red parka.

"Thee'd better hurry up! Thee is *always* late," she says.

"Mom." I stoop down to look her right in the eye at wheel chair level. "That's an old story, and I wish thee would drop it. Please look at me! We're both wonderful, very interesting women over fifty, and I hope thee will be able to see who I am before thee dies!"

Mom coughs. She pulls out her hankie, and says in a soft voice, "Well, that talk thee gave last night at the Peace and Social Justice Committee meeting certainly *was* interesting! Let's hurry up."

We skid backwards down the ramp and get going so fast I am afraid the wheel chair will tip over. Mom then insists on walking the distance to the car with her crutches. I collapse the wheelchair and hoist it into the car trunk, wondering when she will ever let me help her.

The painting studio has large easels, huge paper, and jars of acrylic paint. Today all I can paint is immense fires: red, orange, yellow, and black ashes everywhere. Even though Jonathan has been dead for almost a year and a half, I suddenly remember his body burning in the crematorium. His ashes still sit in our living room. I feel like throwing the paint all over. Instead, I use a fat brush and flame the red and orange all over my canvas.

When I am finished, Mom hobbles over and asks: "Good

Gawd, child, what in the world is that?"

"A huge fire," I answer. "Like the fire that burned down 3,000 houses in the Berkeley-Oakland hills a few years ago." I burst into tears. "Ma—excuse me for crying. Actually, I'm thinking of Jonathan."

Mom's crutches clatter to the floor and she hugs me, sniffling into her sweater.

"I think of him all the time dear. We can cry together."

When we get home from the class, Mom shows me some of her paintings. One in particular surprises me. In the middle of a field filled with large flowers, at the edge of a forest, is something that looks like a red animal with horns.

"Is that a cow? How did thee ever think of making it red?" I ask her.

"I made a mistake," she says. "A big red blob fell right in the middle of my painting! I was so mad I thought I'd throw away the painting. Then I looked again at that large bright blob of red on my canvas, and thought to myself: that looks like a red cow coming out of the forest. So I painted it."

We both burst out laughing.

I Can Say It Out Loud

In the middle of the night, I hear a loud thump, then silence. I jump out of bed and run into Mom's room. Mom and her mattress have slid off the bed together onto the floor. She lies askew, with her one leg on the floor, her amputated leg up in the air. She blinks, dazed.

"Ma, is thee ok? Did thee break anything?"

"I was skiing down the most beautiful fresh powder slope, and I slipped and fell into some rocks," she replied.

"Ma, I think thee was dreaming. Thee's on the floor in thy bedroom, here at home. I'm thy daughter Edie. I'm here next to thee."

Mom stares at me, and then laughs: "Well goodness me. How did I get here?"

At breakfast, Mom asks, "Does thee remember when I took up painting? I think it was after I couldn't ski anymore. But I can't remember when that was. I don't feel old inside, but I look in the mirror and I seem old."

"Ma, thee's eighty-seven. That is old. Thee stopped skiing when thee was eighty-one and thee had thy leg amputated when thee was sixty-eight. Remember? Then thee invited me to join thee at the National Handicapped Ski Center. We took lessons with those little outrigger skis on our poles in the mornings, and practiced racing in the afternoons."

"Thee's clever to remember. That was a long time ago."

"Thee won the National Downhill Handicapped Ski Championship in thy age group. At the awards banquet they gave thee a medal for "The Gutsiest Skier Award.""

"I thought they were teasing me."

"Thee was the oldest competitor on the slope. All the other racers drank beer out of their prostheses and toasted thee at the victory party."

The taxi runs late, and I know there will be heavy traffic on the way to the airport. Mom has laboriously rolled her wheelchair to the front door, leaving her prosthesis leaning against the sofa. She insists on keeping the door open so she can tell me when the taxi arrives. Snow blows onto the plaid blanket covering her legs. I lean down to hug her in her wheelchair.

"Goodbye, Mom. I love thee so much!" I wonder if I will ever see her again.

In a very quiet voice, for the first time, she says: "I love thee, too. I can say it out loud now, because thee's from California!"

Coming Home to a Circle

My mothers' group, which has now morphed into a writing circle, welcomes me back after what may well be my last visit with Mom. We have been meeting every week. I am grateful to be in a circle of women who listen patiently and provide loving witness when sometimes I can only rage at myself, caught again in the sorrow of Jonathan's death. We begin the circle with silence or with music, never with talking. Each week one woman leads the group, offering a poem, a writing exercise using images, or a question invoking memories, and then we write in silence. Finally we each read what we have written. We listen attentively without asking questions. We do not offer criticism, suggestions for improving the writing or questions about how the piece relates to our personal lives. We do not make associations with other literary works or speak of some incident touched off in our own lives. As much as possible we simply "witness" each other.

This deep listening is a potent means to acknowledge each woman's effort to be as authentic as possible. Here we shed all pretense. We are not writing for an audience or for approval. We are writing to dive deep into the well of our own knowing. As we write and listen, we discover how often we have buried these truths in efforts to please, to be successful, even to be spiritual, witty, or artistic. To allow ourselves to strip away layers of conditioning, self-expectations, and above all internal judgments creates an open, sacred space, a sense of ease and freedom. Though we rarely see each other outside of our weekly meetings, I feel intimately connected to each woman, and grateful for her kind listening ears.

I wish that everyone ravaged with grief might have such a circle of homecoming to return to again and again.

Children's Words Consumed By Flames

I just received a letter from Mirsada, my friend from the camp in the Adriatic last summer. She dated the letter February 10th, although I receive it in April. I can hear her voice as I read her letter:

Dear Edie,

Today we received very sad news. The children's paintings and poems were in a car with UNHCR plates, being transported to Sarajevo for the exhibit we have been planning here. Serbs stopped the car just on the other side of the mountains coming into the city. They took everything out of the vehicle and went through each item. When they found the children's paintings, they set them on fire. Not a single one is left!

The snipers fire upon us every day. We have neither water nor electricity. At night I write by candlelight. But I do not burn the rainbow candle you gave me in our woman's circle last summer. It sits on my mantle and gives me hope. I must keep it through the winter. Our warm summer days on Badija Island are far, far away.

Love,

Mirsada.

I have been continuing to give fundraisers for Global Children's Organization so the camps can continue this summer. Now I am so angry, I don't know whether to scream or cry, but when I show slides of the children, the sixteenth century monastery where we lived, the children diving into the clear blue Adriatic, I feel strengthened and inspired again. I am determined to use whatever skills I have to make a difference. I feel very close to my friend Mirsada and to other mothers caught in the web of grief.

Thinking of my friends in Sarajevo, I feel ashamed of my grief. I still have my home and the rest of my family alive and well. Shouldn't I be through grieving by now?

Yet somehow, I sense that patience is important, that I must not run away from my feelings. And I pray that someday I will find a place of serenity and acceptance within myself. Perhaps, then, I will have something useful to offer others.

She Who Remembers

Today my friend Liza brought me a small bamboo cage with three crickets chirping. Long ago in Japan, women brought the first crickets of summer back to the hearth, where they sang to celebrate the silvery languid evenings of summer.

Liza studied music in our living room with Miyo. Our kids go to school together, and we have shared many meals, and kids' concerts since Jonathan's death. How like her to bring such a surprising gift, without talking too much. Many of my friends feel uncomfortable still when they visit and see Jonathan's photograph on the mantle, and I sense their inability to know what to say. How precious are my friends like Liza, who with a simple gift, let me know they still think of Jonathan.

What's Cooking?

The anniversary of Jonathan's death comes in just a few days, and sorrow creeps in again. It's difficult to believe he's been gone for two whole years. I cannot grieve forever. Life calls me back, and I have two beautiful living children. Ben has taken time off from UC Berkeley to travel in Costa Rica. Robin and Keshi are still in school, but I can take a break from concerts and clients, so I join Ben.

When I was just Jonathan's age, I went on my first adventure, to Latin America. Memories of that trip remind me of a time when everything was possible, shining and bright. I lived in a small adobe hut, high on the slopes of Malinche in a Nahuatl village. I woke each morning at dawn to the rooster's clarion call, and to slapping sounds next door, as Maria prepared tortillas for the morning meal. The villagers laughed when I rode my burro down to town for a shower, because my feet almost touched the ground. They nicknamed me "*La Rubia.*" The Blonde.

When I rode down the long arid slopes of the volcano, I heard not a single bus or car, no telephones—nothing but the silence of the immense valley below and the snow-capped vol canoes Ixtaccihuatl and Popocatepetl in the far distance. For the first time in my life, I felt a sublime peace, like music announcing God's presence all around me. I could almost hear the land breathing, seeming to say: 'You are part of me. No need to be afraid ever again.'

The power of this intuition and my delight in working with the villagers sustained me for a decade of work in Latin America before I married. Now, forty years later, what might I rediscover?

I arrive at five a.m. in the San Jose, Costa Rica airport, and Ben isn't there. I have no map, no address and no agenda. Just the youth hostel phone number, which I call.

"Hop on the number sixty-eight Loma Linda bus," Benji says cheerfully. "I'll be waiting for you at the corner of La Loma and Rio Linda. Can't wait to see you!"

An hour later, sure enough, Ben is leaning against a lamppost, whistling. He grabs my backpack as I stumble off the bus. He looks skinny, has his long blond hair tied back in a ponytail and is very tan and grinning.

"I want to take you to my favorite place, a small island off Panama. Bastamientos. The bus leaves in half an hour. We can just make it."

Our little outboard-engine ferry is crammed like a basket

of ripe olives with gorgeous dark healthy men, children and young women. I catch bits of patois sandwiched into a lilting village Spanish as they laugh, drink beer, and throw banana peels into the grimy waters.

Bastamientos is a tiny island, about an hour's drive from Panama City, with no cars, no stores, nothing but warm welcoming Caribbean Panamanians, who greet us the moment we step off the little motorboat.

"*Wappa, man?*" (What happen, man?)

We walk along a path lined with banana trees, bougainvillea, and huge tropical ferns to a small concrete house behind a partially fallen wire fence. Chickens squawk and skitter out of our way as we call through the open doorway.

Ilya welcomes Ben back with a great hug and smile. She has tiny braids tied tight against her head, colored slightly orange. Her smile shines with delight, and she has a calm, intelligent demeanor. Hers is the only inn on the island, and today there is no running water for the toilet or shower. Ben jokes comfortably with Ilya, his lean hulk peering over the counter to sniff what she is cooking for dinner.

I feel immediately as if I've come home. The warmth of Ilya's welcome melts my fatigue. Ilya's welcome is like a great celebration. It is the gladness of a young friend returning, and my own utter delight in seeing my son fold himself into Ilya's plump embrace.

Later Ben ties up my hammock between two palm trees.

"These are really comfortable," he assures me. "You're going to love sleeping here."

I put one leg over the hammock, plop down in the middle and pull up the sides so I won't fall out. I rock back and forth and listen to the chorus of cicadas, the call of the jungle birds, and then the clatter of them settling for the night into papaya and banana trees overhead. Ben is already asleep, curled in his hammock on the other side of the dirt patio.

Half-dozing, I ponder the privilege of being the mother of this young man whose light-filled presence brings joy to everyone around him. Silently I send him my gratitude: *I cannot imagine my life today without you, my wonderful son Ben. You are a miracle and a blessing.*

Haven't You Noticed?

The moon is full and brilliant and I'm so happy to be in a village again that I can't sleep. I smell the sea air and long to go for a swim in the warm salt water. I roll out of the hammock and walk alone into the tropical jungle that borders the island shore; I breathe in the heavy lush air of mosses hanging from the trees. Above the hooded canopy of the forest, I can almost make out the orchids in the moonlight. Ben told me they bloom throughout the year. Amidst such brilliance, could I doubt for a moment that Jonathan's soul lives; that he is here with us now?

The jungle offers a warm soft opening into the earth, like a gigantic vulva. I breathe in an encompassing sensual love, as if the trees and ferns and moss, the flashing color of quetzal, the translucent flicker of hummingbird wings all caress my flesh, slow my breathing, until I stop and cannot speak. No object of my sexuality, no driving need to take, to consummate, to dissolve myself in rapture into someone else.

The jungle creeps right down to the ocean. I drop my clothes on the rocky shore and plunge in to float nude under the full moon in a tide pool, where I rock gently with the waves. No one is here, only me and my aging body. If it will know aches and creaks in the morning, tonight my body is alive and filled with the silence of the Milky Way, the immensity of galaxies spilling out their intelligence. Alone in the tide pool, my ears fill with the music of katydids, parrots, the spray of the ocean. On the eve of Jonathan's death day an immense well-being fills me, as enduring as the warm rolling waves of the Atlantic.

Cool and refreshed, I return and fall asleep instantly in the hammock. Later I awaken from a sound sleep when an intense heat, a white-yellow radiance, pours through me. It holds me in eternal time, safe, forever. There is no need for effort.

I hear a voice clear and sure. It sounds like Jonathan's voice, but it isn't. Something else holds me, fills me with peace. The voice speaks:

"Haven't you noticed? I have been with you all along. Haven't you noticed? I am with you always."

Green Flames of Dawn

First light comes early this morning. Robin is away giving a talk, and I feel like jumping out of bed to greet the day. A full moon slides down behind Mt. Tamalpais, and I can make out the Golden Gate Bridge beyond the bay as morning fog rises. The windows of San Francisco begin to blaze with the rising sun. Time passes a little more quickly now. It is Spring again, more than two years since Jonathan died. I wish Robin were here. I imagine the green flames of dawn in his eyes, the weight of his body, his face unmasked. On an impulse, I send him an email before I go out to walk:

Dearest R: Last night I dreamed of you. I'm still thinking of you this morning. The plum tree is in bloom. Her pink buds swell, eager and plump with longing. She holds her secret still, while her sisters flounce their loveliness – petals of silk cup the sunlight. The green pulse of spring fills her, and like the Jacaranda tree, I drop my purple garments round my roots and wish you were here. Come home soon, love E.

Later I drive to Oakland and play my koto at the Circle of Memories, a stunning memorial for all children who die before their time. Like the Vietnam and Holocaust memorials, the Circle of Memories creates a silent, sacred space for loved ones to remember and to mourn. I am happy to have the opportunity to play music for meditation inside the cave-like structure, made of straw bales, with a single stream falling from the ceiling. I see it as a transparent stream of tears, and then I realize it is salt, falling into a perfect triangular mound on the floor.

The period just before the anniversary of Jonathan's birthday is still a hard time for me. But this year I can play music, sit quietly with other parents, and cry with them as I read messages to their own children. Today I am not thrust into dark despair. I am instead grateful that I can perform music, and I feel close to these parents who are total strangers, whom I will never see again.

Mothers Get Smarter
as They Get Older

Dear Jonathan,

I can't believe it has been so long since I've written you. You'll never guess what I did to celebrate Mother's Day. Remember how terrified I was when you bought your red motorcycle? The day you took Ben for a ride I thought I would die. Well, guess what? Ben just got a big yellow Honda 580. He has a yellow helmet, yellow jacket, leather boots, and thick yellow leather gloves. He looks like a gigantic yellow bumblebee. When he invited me out for a ride as a Mother's Day present, I decided that I'd get over my nervousness by taking a ride with him. I'm sure you're laughing as you read this. Don't you wish even a little bit that you were here to ride with us?

Ben gave me a helmet, showed me how to pull it down tight and strap it on, and then he helped me mount up behind him. He drove slowly up and down Contra Costa Ave., teaching me how to lean forward, put my hands on his hipbones instead of clutching him around the waist, and how to lean with him going around the curves. He took me straight up steep Marin Ave., until I thought I would slide off backwards.

When we got into Tilden Park I calmed down and began to enjoy myself. The smell of eucalyptus trees filled the air, and I could see all the way over to Mt. Diablo as we rode to the very top of the park. We wound down the sharp hairpin turns to the lake in Briones Park. I loved swooping around the sharp turns, leaning way over, feeling the wind against my cheeks. And I wasn't scared in the least.

I think I finally understand what fun you had that summer when you rode with your friends all over the back roads in Marin. Too bad I wasn't brave enough to ride with you. Were you laughing this afternoon as we roared through the park and I hollered to the wind?

—Your Mom

Cats

Dear Jonathan,

Benji is taking time out from college, just the way you did, and is working at a software company in the "Silicon Valley" of San Francisco. Soon he will be the same age you were when you died! Have you been watching over him?

Are you purring with big brother pride to see him now? Or maybe you've been guiding him all along. He's followed in your footsteps in many ways, even though you two are so very different.

After Benji graduated from high school, he worked as a ski lift operator, then got a job in a small computer company that reminded me a little of Berkeley Systems — hip and no one over thirty in the company. They make screen-savers too, and Benji got his name on one program that I love as much as the flying toasters you designed. Its called Cats!

Cats is an interactive screen saver, so you can pat the cute little meowser and he'll purr, or give him catnip and he races around the screen, and then rolls in ecstasy on his back; or feed him with a bottle of milk when he meows and he'll curl up, tail around his nose, for a nap.

Did you see him that evening when the power went out in San Francisco? Just when Ben's team needed to meet the deadline for Cats? I'm sure you laughed uproariously as you saw them walk down six flights of stairs carrying their computers, then three blocks through the blackened streets to a company that had its own generator. They finished the program and met their deadline. Ben—that's what everyone calls him now—arrived home baggy-eyed and triumphant. Remind you of yourself?

We all miss you so much, dear Jonathan. These days, I feel saddest for Ben. I sense how close you are still, how much you remain a part of our lives. Much love to you.

—Your Mom

P e r s i m m o n s

Dear Jonathan,

This year we harvested the very first and only persimmon from your memorial garden. It reminded me again of fall in Kyoto with the lanterns of orange persimmons shining against the black tiles of the temple roofs.

Your garden is a great gift to me. Every time I walk in it, pick flowers, and pull weeds, I think of you and of all our friends who donated plants to remember you. The garden brings me a deep feeling of equanimity. We still haven't scattered the last of your ashes, Jonathan. I think perhaps I am ready to lay them to rest here.

Jonathan, you have been helping me in so many ways. I hope you still watch me, can still hear me, and know how grateful I am for your life, for what you are teaching me with your death. I carry you now inside me, like a bright burning ember, like a meadow, like a song.

—Your Mom

Giving Away His Gold

Nothing makes me lose it like the computer.

It's just a machine; I try to calm my rising feeling of help-lessness. *Calm down. You've handled much more difficult situations than this.* The computer seems to have a malevolent purpose all its own. *This has nothing to do with me. It does not prove I'm incompetent.* The screen goes blank and seems to gobble up one of my files. I want to pull the plug and throw the wretched tormentor out the window.

Instead I call Ben, trying to mask my frustration.

"Hey Ben, I'm having a problem with the computer. Do you have time to come over this weekend?"

Half an hour later, fully recovered from his sleepless nights completing *Cats*, Ben hugs me at the front door.

"Actually I was planning to come over and do some laundry today. Would you like a lesson for the technologically challenged?" We both laugh.

"Oh, by the way, I made some toll house cookies to celebrate the launching of Cats. Want some?"

As Ben turns on the computer I go to the kitchen and start preparing supper, feeling less at the mercy of my disobedient machine while I'm cooking.

"Ben," I call into the study "I can't keep up with my email. My friends all complain that I don't answer their invitations. Any smart ideas?"

"They should call you on the phone. Tell them you're voice activated."

"You're a genius," I laugh.

In amazement and delight I bask in the presence of my wonderful son. Like a shaft of sunlight, Ben gives his gold away for the pure pleasure of kindness.

Like a Song Riding the Wind

Dear Jonathan,

I haven't written you in such a long time! Ben's back at UC Berkeley again, and Keshi will graduate from high school in a week. Imagine—next fall she's off to college. Which means she's been a member of our family for seven years. And you've been gone for four years.

Sometimes I still wonder—what would you be doing now if you'd stuck around? Would you still be so single-minded? Maybe into the "dot-com" world in Silicon Valley? Somehow I doubt it— probably you'd be inventing with other computer nerds, or maybe you would have decided to go to college. I guess it's silly to speculate, but I can't help imagining.

Last weekend, we held our annual Memorial Day fundraiser in your honor. We raised enough money for Keshi's trip to work with the refugee children in Croatia this summer. We'll travel together to study with Thich Nhat Hanh again in France for a week and then she'll work with the children in Sarajevo and I will work with women there.

As part of the fundraiser, Ben and Keshi played the Schubert *Death and the Maiden* that Ben played at your public memorial service at the Quaker Meeting House. I still cry every time I hear it! I hope you don't mind. These days my tears are not so much of sadness as recognition—that you really have left us forever, at least as the young man you were. And also, a new kind of acceptance creeps into my bones—some new glimmer of understanding about the sorrow and joy that makes up the fabric of our lives. I can imagine that from where you are these thoughts and emotions seem like passing clouds, like a song riding the wind, which of course they are.

I am beginning to feel a little like my old self. Sometimes I wonder if I'm betraying you by feeling happiness again. Then I remember what Kay said one day when I cried:

"Edie—Jonathan's spirit will never be free if you keep on crying. He isn't able to completely leave because of your sadness. You have to let him go."

I'm sure she's right. And I do want your spirit to be free. I just hope you know how much I still miss you, even when I enjoy myself. I love you and miss you.

—Your coming-back-to-life-Mom

Learning to Sing in my New Nest

This morning I wake up at five-thirty and cannot get back to sleep. Maybe it's the excitement of Keshi's graduation. Walking down the wooden stairwell I stop at the butsudan to ring the bell, light incense, and speak with Miyo.

Miyo—are you still watching over us? Can you believe that Keshi actually graduates from high school today? Her classmates have chosen her to give the farewell speech, and she's going to wear your niece Sumi's kimono. I hope I can tie the obi correctly! And how I wish you were here with us.

It seems only an instant ago that you were so sick and we said goodbye. And here's Keshi all grown up. Thank you, dear Miyo. What a gift you have given us. You and Keshi have both helped me in so many ways.

By mid-afternoon, the air is scorching hot in Marin, and even though I wear a wide brimmed hat and summer dress, I am dripping. Robin takes off his jacket. Keshi must be dying in that kimono, I think. Ben wears a silk shirt, vest, black felt hat, linen pants and his Tevas. Our extended family and friends all sit with bouquets of flowers in the third row.

Keshi walks, with calm dignity, up to the podium. The long sleeves of her bright yellow and red chrysanthemum and plum blossom kimono flutter beside her. I cry throughout her talk and just about burst with pride. Soon I will be saying goodbye to her. This summer she'll study with Thich Nhat Hanh and then go to work with the refugee children in Croatia. In the fall, she'll leave home to go to college. Keshi ends her farewell to the school and to her classmates with a poem, which has meant a lot to her, by Thich Nhat Hanh:

Do not say I depart tomorrow
because even today I still arrive.
Look deeply: I arrive in every second
to be a bud on a spring branch,
to be a tiny bird, with wings still fragile,
learning to sing in my new nest.

That night I have a dream: I am paddling in a canoe with Keshi down a New England river in the summer. Maple, oak, and pine trees line the banks of the river, along with blueberry bushes, all of them full and lush. We pick blueberries in handfuls off the bushes as we pause for a moment. The water is somewhat green, murky from all the leaves that settled during the winter. Keshi and I do not speak, but paddle with no effort, each echoing the rhythm of the other. We have just returned from our work in Sarajevo, and neither of us gives directions.

My daughter is no longer a child. She has grown to a young woman. We paddle with equal strength in silence. The late orange afternoon sunlight streams through the forest, abuzz with katydids. Two dragonflies glide inches above the water, locked together. The summer sun has filled my body to the brim. I bathe in a green shade. Time stops. Words are unnecessary.

I lie awake for a long time, remembering Keshi's talk and poem. She could have been speaking for me, as I turn sixty, as I also step over a threshold, as I acknowledge the end of this phase of my life with children living at home. I, too, am still arriving. I now know, as surely as I have experienced love's radiance, that I will die and that death is not the end of the soul's journey.

Jonathan Sends a Dream

A week later I have another dream, this time of Jonathan. I awaken filled with a sense of light, of warmth all over my body and of peace, as if bathed in sunlight. I exist in a completely silent place, a desert perhaps—no bird sound, no wind, only bright sunlight all over my body.

I am with Jonathan and we chat happily, relaxed, enjoying each other's company. We just celebrated my Quaker grandmother Bema's birthday—on August 7th. Jonathan expresses surprise that I know the date, and asks, "How did you know?"

"There are seven pomegranate seeds on the ground in front of us. That is how I know," I say.

We both laugh with the pleasure of the alchemical number and understand without saying more.

"I just love being with you. You are such a wonderful person. I love you," I say. We laugh and kiss each other. He kisses me gently on the lips.

"I love you, too," he says. The kiss comes as from an angelic being, an apparition, like an angel on a Renaissance chapel, surrounded by clouds, and youthful innocence—not sexual, but a light brush of the lips. Not sweet and sentimental. A child's kiss, just full of dearness. I feel a divine joy, unlike anything I have ever felt here on earth. His hug is firm and present, not hesitant or withdrawing. Just there, together with me in a matter-of-fact kind of way. Tears sting in my eyes.

"I wish you were still alive so we could enjoy each other in life this way. Do you ever wish you were back in life again?"

With tears in his eyes, he says, "No."

I understand immediately. "You're much happier now aren't you? The way it is here?"

"Yes," he says, "it is much more beautiful here. I wouldn't want to come back."

I understand completely, feel a boundless, empty yet blessed peacefulness, a deep contentment. In this spacious realm where Jonathan is now, there is no struggle, no conflict, no yearning of the heart for anything else.

I wake with a great heat throughout my body, feeling stunned, as if finally I do understand. How beautiful. How unspeakably exquisite. What a precious visit.

It is only now, here, returning to thinking, that I begin to feel pain and sorrow again, as I wish I could change his death and bring him back or be with him as I was in the dream. It is the longing, the attachment to my wish to change things that causes me pain, not the dream, or the visitation, not even the fact of his death.

Jonathan, you are radiantly happy and peaceful. Thank you for this beautiful glimpse into our true nature, our capacity to love. Thank you for this brief moment of pure being with you, for this vision of death, this glimpse of liberation.

The Mendelssohn Trio

This year, on the anniversary of Jonathan's death, I do not weep. The pain doesn't cease, but it begins to separate from me and become more encased, like a thorn, or perhaps a deeply buried grain of sand, smooth and luminous as a pearl, alongside so much gratitude.

Ben and Keshi come home from college over Christmas break. Their gift to Robin and me on our wedding anniversary reads:

Chef Keshi and Chef Ben

invite you to

an evening of

delectable dining

for two

at

Chez Hartshorne-Brooks

on the

evening of your choice.

Menu by request

or

Chef's choice

In front of the fire, they serve us wine and cheese while preparing sorrel watercress soup, shrimp with tart apples, snow peas, mustard, and crème fraiche; artichokes stuffed with Italian sausage, and homemade fresh apple pie.

After dinner Keshi says, "Let's play the Mendelssohn trio."

"What cellist could resist that slow movement?" Ben says. He takes his cello from the case, adjusts the floor peg and settles himself, glancing up at Robin and Keshi. Robin sounds an A on the piano while Ben and Keshi both tune up. All three sit quietly for a moment making eye contact. Ben takes a breath, lifts his bow and with a sound as delicate as the wind he slips into the first liquid phrases of the andante with Robin accompanying him. A few measures later Keshi makes her entrance and I stretch out on the rug next to the living room fireplace.

I can just see the tufts of Robin's bird-nest hair waving slightly with the beat, above the music stand of the piano. As rain pours down the windowpanes, I close my eyes, allow the music to wash over me, put a pillow under my head and curl up on the Oriental rug, close to heaven.

Dare I write of such happiness? Am I tempting the great weaver to snip another thread of my life if I cherish these tender moments again? If I acknowledge that I am woven into wholeness by love's golden threads?

Would I trade this joy and freedom for Jonathan's life, if magically I could bargain with death? The question now seems irrelevant. Redoing the past or longing for the future only pierces my heart with pain. Instead I celebrate my blessings and am filled with gratitude. My life is an abundance of joy and sorrow, a blessing from every drop of rain and every ray of sunlight, from every kindness, each family member and each friend.

The fire crackles, calls me back to Mendelssohn's luscious phrases and the pleasure of my family playing music together. Remembering a fragment from the psalms, I speak silently to an abiding presence of divinity in my life, and to Jonathan:

You have changed my grieving into dancing!
Thrown off my mourning clothes and
    dressed me in joy
So that my whole being might sing to you
    without ceasing
Pouring out my gratitude without end.

I know now that suffering can transform into light, shining through blue shadows at dawn, that love is more enduring than death.

Acknowledgements

Mending With Gold

A precious Japanese tea bowl, when broken, is always mended with gold.

Shortly after Jonathan died, my friend Susan Felix, a ceramic artist, brought me an exquisite, pit-fired bowl. Flames had burnished it black. "To contain your blessings," she said.

That night when I couldn't sleep, I lay on the sofa and gazed at the bowl. Later, I awoke with a start and brushed against the bowl with the sleeve of my bathrobe. Like a dark blossom it fell, opening into four pieces on the rug. Susan came by the next day with her gold glue.

"It will become like you," she said. "More beautiful for the brokenness."

Today my blessing bowl does indeed overflow. Dozens of people have supported the completion of this book, each in his or her individual way.

Special thanks to Wes Boyd, Joan Blades, Ben Resner, Jack Eastman and all the folks at Berkeley Systems who enabled Jonathan to flourish.

For sustenance and love in the hardest times, as well as the most joyful: Patricia and Daniel Ellsberg, Enid Schreibman, Nicole Milner, Susan Felix, Sandra Lewis, Patrice Wynne, Judith Jenya, Claire Ullman, Judy Kranzler-Wyrobek, Iris Ratowsky, Liza and Michael Dalby, Nersi and Bella Ramazan-nia, Dave and Kay Werdegar, Suzanne Palmer Lovell, Anne Reed, Sarah Carey and Jack Reilly, Curry Barber, Dori Draper.

For providing sacred space, and writing circles: Sherry Anderson and the Tuesday group; my Mothers' Circle: Judith Thomas, Nancy Herrick, Mia Hachem, Judith Tripp, Susan Jaffe; for offering wisdom, great food, and kindness, as well as writing insights: Sheilah Glover, Elaine Belle, Barbara Borden, Suzanne West.

To my artist and musician colleagues, who helped me continue to create and believe that the arts can transform hearts and inspire peace, *especially* in hard times: Mayumi Oda, Kaz Tanahashi, Pamela Meidel, Paloma Pavel and Richard Page, Claire Greensfelder, Wendy Oser, Nicole Milner, PhoeBe ANNE sorgen, Betsy Rose, Jennifer Berezan, Gael Alcock, Barbara Borden, Naomi Neuman, Shielah Glover, Judith-Kate Friedman, Arisika Razak, Evelie Posch, Catherine Allport, Kathleen Sweeney, Lisa Rafel, Judy Fjell, Karl Linn, Adam Miller, Janet Bray, Rashani,

Rafael Gonzales, Doug Von Koss, Avacha, and Lee Mun Wah.

I thank Mary Oliver and Naomi Shihab Nye whose poems have inspired and sustained me. Thanks also to Norman Fischer for his beautiful translation of the Psalms.

For spiritual direction Thich Nhat Hanh, Sister Chan Khong, Sylvia Boorstein, Jack Kornfield, Yvonne Rand and Janet Adler.

For wise mentoring and editorial help: Manuela Dunn-Mascetti, Betsy Blakeslee, Anita Barrows, Sue Bender, Susan Page, Sandy Boucher, and Michael Ellsberg.

I would also like to thank Jerrry Karzen, Skeeter and my colleagues in the Hawaii Feldenkrais Training Program.

For financial support, I thank the Lyman Fund and Charlotte Fardelmann.

I am grateful for thoughtful reading and comments from all those who endorsed the book. My heartfelt thanks for continuing support and encouragement from Jan Sells, Hank Swan, Verona Fonte, Linda Hess, Caroline North, Karen Miller, Lynn Fine, Terry Mandell, Joan Marler and Dan Smith, Lowell Brook, Shoshana Cole, Barbara and Ed Tonningsen, Kristine Maltrud, Jodi Gold, Peggy Hackney, Mercy Sidbury, Lee Morgan, Meg Porter Alexander, Cynthia Jurs, Abigail Alling, Cynthia Lazaroff, Susan Werner, Joan Lester, Harriet Hope, Vivian Verdan-Roe, Barbara Zilber, Anne and John Watt, Suzanne Pearce, Lill Kemp, Coco and Kyra Montagu, Mary Neuman, Linda Braun, Jayn

Rosenfeld Siegel, Penny Adams, Frinde Maher, Ellen Schrecker, Andy Towl, John Pappenheimer, Sarah Hull, Sana Roy Sears, Penny Gwinn Vestner, Elinor Horner, Lisa Eustis, Analise Rigan.

My Churchill family of origin, Hal, Fred, Ellen, their spouses Diana, Margot, John and their children kept me connected to my Yankee roots, even at a great distance. I am especially grateful to my twin brother Hal Churchill and his wife Diana Post who know the heartbreak of losing a child. Thanks also to our Hartshorne families, especially Marianna Hartsong and Cary Flanagan. My intrepid mother, Posie Churchill, is with me in spirit, though she passed two years ago. I give thanks for her determination, sense of adventure, delight in learning and zest for life. In Ecuador, where I now work with indigenous peoples, I sleep in a tree house called "*Casa Mama Posie*" in her honor. She'd be delighted.

For her artistic eye and elegant design I thank Kate Canfield. Thanks also to Erin Sickler for her initial design ideas and her enthusiasm. Nomi Wanag and Nicole Becker and Dennis Rivers offered invaluable assistance.

I am beholden to Nicholas Kirsten-Honshin for his beautiful print, on the cover of this book. Thanks also to Krystal Kirsten.

Warm thanks to Pearl Luke, my kind and generous editor; her keen editorial eye and patient teaching has greatly enhanced this book.

I could never have imagined a more wonderful agent than Jill Kneerim. Her humanity, sense of humor, wit and intelligence carried this book from its raw beginnings to completion.

My dear friend Vijali Hamilton, sculptor, musician, peace activist and spiritual mentor has inspired me in every area of my life. She is the *Madrina* (Godmother) of this book. I thank her also for reuniting me with a love of my youth: working with indigenous peoples in Latin America.

The love and support I received from my two living children, Ben and Keshi, and my husband, Robin, provided the "ground of being" for this book. I thank them for their many blessings: Ben for his kindness, patience, integrity, and computer wizardry. His generous, open heart dazzles me and continues to affirm my belief in the goodness of life. Keshi for her courage and strength, for beauty in all she touches, and for her commitment to social justice. She inspires my own courage and broadens my life. My delight in the gift of a daughter is boundless and I thank her parents, Ethan and Miyo Brooks for entrusting their dearest treasure to us.

Robin for sharing the challenges and wonder of our children's lives, and most of all, for living his beliefs. His steady love, discerning intelligence and special quality of "presence" have sustained and inspired me. This book is his story as well as mine.

About the Author

Edie Hartshorne, MSW, is a therapist, musician and writer. Raised a Quaker and now a practicing Buddhist, she integrates spiritual inquiry and music with her therapeutic private practice. She is also a Guild Certified Feldenkrais Practitioner.

As a musician she has performed extensively in the US, Europe, Latin America and Japan; at Buddhist events, retreats with Thich Nhat Hahn, and at the Dalai Lama Sacred Music Festival. In recognition of her work using music for peace she was elected a Fellow of the World Academy of Art and Science.

A former Fulbright Scholar in Uruguay and advocate for indigenous people in Latin America, she currently collaborates with the World Wheel to preserve indigenous Shuar culture and the rainforest in Ecuador. She is also Co-Director of A World Without Armies: Costa Rica Initiative.

A recipient of the Distinguished Women of Berkeley Award, she lives with her husband in Berkeley, CA and is the mother of two grown children. You can contact Edie by email at edie@hartshorne.net; her web page is http://edie.hartshorne.net.

Additional copies of this book can be ordered at:
www.lightinblueshadows.com
or at Amazon and other online bookstores

53175602R00143

Made in the USA
Columbia, SC
13 March 2019